ESSAYS IN PHILOSOPHY AND EDUCATION

Laurence J. Stott
University of Toronto

UNIVERSITY
PRESS OF
AMERICA

Lanham • New York • London

Copyright © **1988** by

University Press of America,® Inc.

4720 Boston Way
Lanham, MD 20706

3 Henrietta Street
London WC2E 8LU England

Printed in the United States of America

British Cataloging in Publication Information Available

Library of Congress Cataloging-in-Publication Data

Stott, Laurence J., 1935–
Essays in philosophy and education / Laurence J. Stott.
p. cm.
Includes bibliographies.
1. Education—Philosophy. 2. Philosophy. I. Title.
LB41.S789   1988
370'.1—dc 19   88–14763 CIP
ISBN 0–8191–7039–9 (alk. paper)
ISBN 0–8191–7040–2 (pbk. : alk. paper)

All University Press of America books are produced on acid-free
paper which exceeds the minimum standards set by the National
Historical Publications and Records Commission.

To Mum, Dad and Di

Acknowledgements

I wish to acknowledge my debt to Professor Donald Vandenburg. He initiated me into the excitement of philosophy, a move I have rarely had cause to regret.

Table of Contents

Preface

I hope this book will be read as a unity, not merely dipped into for this or that particular essay; the order of essays is not inconsequential.

It is perhaps doubtful whether any individual can liberate him(her) self from most of the beliefs and values 'caught' during childhood; because of childhood vulnerability we are all victims, to one degree or another, of time and place of birth. If there is an escape route it is in philosophy, poetry and literature. Here, in the liberal arts, our most basic assumptions and most cherished beliefs are challenged and often undermined. The study of philosophy is best conceived as an exposure to a sustained and direct attack on ways of thinking and feeling: each philosophy claims to give one the right handle on life. The 'attack' in poetry and literature is generally less direct, but no less disturbing.

It is unfortunate that philosophy is so often viewed as academic and impractical. It is academic only in the exemplary sense of being thoughtful and consistent, and it is impractical only to the degree that we reject this or that philosophy. A philosophy is best thought of as a pattern of beliefs and values embodied in the lives of individuals. All the world religions bear testimony to the fact that philosophy is living and 'practical'.

Is there any natural linkage between philosophy and education, or is it merely tradition that philosophy is given a nod in teacher training programs? I think the tightest link resides in their common purpose—to inform and enlarge mental, and emotional, horizons. Teachers who have not questioned their own philosophies are hardly fit to be let loose on young people of differing philosophies. The educator, perforce, needs to be well educated.

This book is presented to all who take seriously the task of raising children. Teachers are second in importance only to parents. Wisdom only deepens with age.

By "man" I shall always mean "humankind".

...this life is teaching. ...This life is presented, then, to those who come later, to teach them not what is and must be, but how life is lived in the spirit, face to face with the Thou. That is, it is itself ready on every occasion to become Thou for them, and open up the world of Thou—no; it is not ready: it continually approaches and touches them. But they, having become disinclined and unfitted for the living dealings that would open the world to them, are fully equipped with information. They have pinned the person down in history, and secured his words in the library. They have codified, in exactly the same way, the fulfilment or the breaking of the law. Nor are they niggards with admiration and even idolatry, amply mixed with psychology, as befits modern man. O lonely Face like a star in the night, O living Finger laid on an unheeding brow, O fainter echoing footstep!

MARTIN BUBER

Chapter 1

Philosophy a Frill?

Given the continuing fiscal squeeze on faculties of education, programs are being reassessed and all courses are being scrutinized. Which courses can be eliminated without detracting seriously from the quality of teacher preparation programs?

Philosophy of education courses are increasingly being viewed as impractical, an academic frill one can excise with scant loss to teacher preparation programs, (though, it may be conceded, such courses might well be useful at the graduate level). I wish to take this view seriously. Trying to capture the essence of the charge, I restate the view as follows: Philosophy is an ivory tower pursuit, which is to say that philosophers read, think and talk rather than conduct field research. Thus philosophy is removed from the fray. Teaching is fray. Therefore philosophy is impractical and of little or no utility in a teacher preparation program.

The phrase "philosophy of education" is open to various interpretations which, in the end, reflect differing views regarding the function of philosophy within teacher education. One's stand is, in the final analysis, a value judgement, a statement of what philosophy of education ought, in the main, to be aiming at. This statement will, however, like all ought statements, be constrained by the historical meaning load carried by words, that is, "philosophy" cannot mean anything at all I please, and neither can "education". I wish to make a clear statement regarding what, in my view, philosophy of education courses should, in the main, be aiming at, and then to defend such courses against the charges of impracticality and non-utility.

Philosophy has always been concerned with questions of value, with the good (and with the true and the beautiful to the extent to which these can be classified as value questions), and in wrestling with such questions, philosophers invariably have found themselves driven to notions of the nature of man. To eliminate such questions from philosophy is to eliminate the soul of traditional philosophy. To those who regard such surgery as a step forward, I

have to say that value questions are clearly primary since the style
of individual lives, and of societies, is at stake. Moreover, I believe
one can make significant headway with value issues if one is willing
to take seriously the notion "the nature of man", its vagueness
notwithstanding.

I here accept 'wrestling with value questions' as a major concern of philosophy, and here assert that wrestling with the problem of ultimate aims, and consequent key features, of education
should be the major concern of philosophy of education.[1] Put
simply, my view is that philosophy of education courses should
force student teachers to consider what schooling should pursue,
what it should add up to in the lives of students, and hence what
key features should characterize schooling. Thus all lesson notes
and all curricula decisions could be finally justified, shaped and
made sense of, by overriding aims and features, which in turn
would be grounded in a thoughtful view of the nature of man. Are
such courses ivory tower, impractical, and of little or no utility in a
teacher preparation program?

Philosophy, in my view, is indeed ivory tower: philosophers
read, think and talk rather than engage in field research. To this
extent it is out of the fray. Philosophy is indeed impractical in that
it does not issue in precise instructions on how to conduct the
Monday 9:00 a.m. mathematics grade eight fray; philosophy
operates not at the nitty gritty level of day-to-day specific problems, but at a higher value/principle level. Moreover, in my view,
philosophy does not issue in demonstrably final answers to the
questions of value it does tackle; rather it gives clarity and some
precision to difficult choices, to dilemmas and to limits of knowing. Furthermore, I maintain that one can teach school mathematics, typing, chemistry and such very well without having
engaged in formal philosophy. Philosophy is also impractical
inasmuch as aims and key features of schooling are laid down by
government departments of education so the questions have
already been answered, pro tem, by qualified others. So, to the
extent that teachers are bound by government and school policies, the individual teacher cannot implement his/her own
answers anyway. Philosophy is also impractical in that it hardly
constitutes a qualification destined to assure success and advance-
ment within the school system: questioning ultimate aims and key
features tends to upset rather than impress those in authority.

Given all the above, the charges of impracticality and non-
utility should not be dismissed lightly. I wish to insist, however,
that such impracticalities notwithstanding, philosophy of education courses are essential within teacher preparation programs,

that the senses in which they are practical is of such import to the welfare of the school system as to reduce to triviality the senses in which they are not.

To be a child is to be taught to play a cultural game (I do not use the word "game" pejoratively). The rules and point of the game become clearly known: what counts as a win, as a loss, as fair, as foul, as laudable, who qualifies as referee, who blows the whistle, etc. The school inevitably reflects and supports, to high degree, the current cultural game. The child becomes embroiled in the game and plays it to the best of his ability. Socialization is ubiquitous and inevitable.

Philosophy is ivory tower, out-of-the-social-fray, reflecting. But this ivory tower is of a particular sort. It is best thought of as a spotter's box high above the football stadium. The spotter is undoubtedly out of the fray, but his vantage point gives him a perspective on the game that the players could not possibly achieve. He will be able to see, and judge, patterns of play that those caught up in the heat of the game cannot see. Pushing the analogy to its limits, reflecting on the nature of the game, and of its players, the spotter could conceivably conclude that the game was not worth playing, that life should have higher purpose than chasing a ball and seeking to outplay others. This new-found view, born of the distance his tower afforded him, will affect how he conducts himself 'back' in the world.

Philosophy is the call, indeed the demand, to reflect on life and the social game one was inducted into, to gain distance on it. Is it really worth playing? Could it be played differently, better? The pursuit of truth, beauty, goodness inevitably puts a cultural game into question, just as it puts a personal life style into question. Philosophy is not concerned with success within the current game. Philosophy of education is concerned with whether or not, or to what degree, we ought to play the current schooling game; whether or not the current aims and chief features of schooling are right and good (and, possibly, true and beautiful).

So whilst philosophy is out of the fray, to baldly term it impractical seems particularly stupid. The man in the spotter's box is not escaping life; he is not contemplating his navel nor is he hypnotized by swirling clouds. He is in the serious business of getting a clear view of the game, in reflecting on that game, and at stake are people's life styles; he is in the serious business of reflecting on the school game, of judging its overall aims and effects and its pervading key features, and at stake is how we influence the young, what sort of game we embroil them in. He will 'take back' with him his new-found view.

So the question is whether or not student teachers should be able to, or have to, reflect on the nature of the schooling game, and its participants, before being caught up in the game such that their perspective is unavoidably squeezed.

A large number of student teachers see no virtue in entering the school system unquestioning of its aims and key features. It is a stubborn fact that intelligent people do question, insist on questioning. To deny these people the opportunity for such reflection is surely inexcusable, certainly within a university, and doubly so within a democracy. And those students who see no virtue in considering ultimate aims and main features of schooling should surely be made to ponder. Do we really wish to have our children taught by provincial-minded teachers? Should student teachers not be made aware that they are embarking upon a moral enterprise, with all the difficulties and dilemmas that poses?

The practical import of engaging in serious philosophical reflection lies in the effect it has on attitude. To hold to certain values, whether or not one has reflected on them, and whether or not one can articulate them, is to have a philosophy. One's attitude to the world and people is the concrete reflection of one's values and hence of one's philosophy. A teacher's attitude to life, to school, to people, will pervade the classroom and children will bear the brunt of it for good or ill. By raising the question of values, along with the assumptions, hidden or otherwise, that are involved, philosophy of education bears on deep-seated attitudes. By bringing into focus and scrutinizing different views of the nature of man, with attendant value patterns and hence aims and key features of education, students' views are challenged and attitudes invariably softened. More so, I think, than any other discipline, philosophy tends to humbling, tends to wisdom. The commitment that ensues is sincere and informed rather than fanatical. Since a teacher's attitude colours all his/her dealings with children, and since attitude escapes legislative policies (when the classroom door is shut I am very much the king), it is better that our children be taught by the wise rather than by the narrow, by the thoughtful rather than by the shrill. Expertise in teaching a subject is not enough; the medium of a teacher's classroom teaches more, and more deeply, than the message.

Consider, for example, the philosophy of Friedrich Nietzsche.[2] The cultural game Nietzsche found himself embroiled in was calling for certain plays: Christian love-thy-neighbour plays, democratic anti-elitist respect-everyone plays, and statism be-a-good (obedient)-citizen plays. From the vantage point of his psychic spotter's box, Nietzsche reflected upon the game he and others were being pressured to play and judged it foolheaded. Everywhere he looked in nature he saw the struggle for power-vitality. Some trees made the light and flourished, others were crowded out and shrivelled; some people are strong-creative, others are weak-conforming. There is health and there is sickness. Being convinced that man was part of nature, that life was the will to power and that God was dead, Nietzsche concluded that elitism was not merely inevitable, it was good; the nature of man was to be caught up in the struggle for power-vitality and the point of life was 'overcoming', was power-creativity. To hold down the strong-creative would be to institute social decay.

> Refraining mutually from injury, violence and exploitation and placing one's will on a par with that of someone else—this may become, in a certain rough sense, good manners among individuals if the appropriate conditions are present (namely, if these men are actually similar in strength and value standards and belong together in one body). But as soon as this principle is extended, and possibly even accepted as the fundamental principle of society, it immediately proves to be what it really is—a will to the denial of life, a principle of disintegration and decay. (Nietzsche, 1966. p. 203)

Thus anti-elitist, respect-everyone, love-everyone plays were anti-life, were attempts to level, to share power rather than concentrate it in the hands of the strong-creative, to condemn the struggle for power.[3] The strong-creative have no motive for being sadistic, and graciousness is the mark of one who has "attained his height and rules" (Nietzsche, 1966. p. 222) but nevertheless, societies exist for the strong, not for the weak. To live is to exploit. To use the weak is inevitable and right. For the strong to love the weak as a matter of policy would be insane. For the strong to respect the weak would make no sense.

> The essential characteristic of a good and healthy aristocracy, however, is that it experiences itself not as a function (whether of the monarchy or the commonwealth) but as their meaning and highest justification—that it therefore accepts with a good conscience the sacrifice of untold human beings who, for its sake, must be reduced and lowered to incomplete human beings, to slaves, to instruments. Their fundamental faith simply has to be that society must not exist for society's sake but only as the foundation and scaffolding on which a choice type of being is able to raise itself to its higher task... (p. 202)

> Even the body within which individuals treat each other as equals, as suggested before—and this happens in every

healthy aristocracy—if it is a living and not a dying body, has to do to other bodies what the individuals within it refrain from doing to each other: it will strive to grow, spread, seize, become predominant—not from any morality or immorality but because it is living and because life simply is will to power. But there is no point on which the ordinary consciousness of Europeans resists instruction as on this: everywhere people are now raving, even under scientific disguises, about coming conditions of society in which "the exploitative aspects" will be removed—which sounds to me as if they promised to invent a way of life that would dispense with all organic functions. "Exploitation" does not belong to a corrupt or imperfect and primitive society; it belongs to the essence of what lives, as a basic organic function; it is a consequence of the will to power, which is after all the will of life.

If this should be an innovation as a theory—as a reality it is the primordial fact of all history; people ought to be honest...(p. 203)

The consequences of such a philosophy upon one's conception of education and schooling are indeed dramatic. The ultimate aim of life will prescribe the ultimate aim of education, namely, that the strong-creative rise to the top within the school and within the society. The main feature of any classroom will reflect the ultimate aim of education, and in the case of this particular philosophy, the main feature of life, namely, struggle.

The teacher of this persuasion teaches to the bright students, driving them relentlessly to the far reaches of their abilities. To teach is to constantly challenge, to learn is to constantly strive. The teacher will be totally uncompromising with regard to standards. To sell short the bright student is to be anti-life. Some students will get hurt along the way, being unable to keep up, but this teacher will not relent, neither will he be upset. The weak will always get hurt. Teach them enough so that later on they will be of some use to the strong-creative, but understand that they are of no moment. The aim of teaching is clear: that the strong-creative flourish; the function of the school system is clear: to separate out the strong from the weak. To teach to the average student, to let standards drift downward so that none need fail, is to institute social decay.

The teacher of this persuasion understands the necessity to be in command. If the teacher does not take power in the classroom, someone else will—not because that someone is moral or immoral, but because (s)he is alive, because life is the will to power, and because (s)he is evidently stronger, more dynamic, than the teacher is. The teacher does not respect all his students, only the strong-creative, but he demands respect from all. He does not love all his students—he loves whom he finds he loves—and does not seek love. His task is to drive the capable to be ever more proficient, the creative to be ever more creative. The stakes are high. The school is no place for sentimentality.

The elitist attitude of such a teacher will pervade every class, and students will bear the brunt of it. Attitude is all bound up with one's conceptions of ultimate aims and consequent values, which in turn flow from, or assume, a conception of the nature of man. Thus philosophy structures attitude.

Philosophy of education courses bring such philosophies into the light of day and argue the validity of them. There are no privileged positions in philosophy, neither are there forbidden positions. The quest for truth is without fear or favour. Pat answers are shown to be so. Such courses are a constant and vivid reminder to the student teacher that teaching is a moral, not merely technical, enterprise. The process of weighing positions is a maturing process, as liberating as it is discomfiting; to engage in philosophy is to be battered as much as it is to be enlightened. Philosophy is scornful only of mindlessness, of uncritical acceptance.

Whether we like it or not, philosophy is the heart and soul of human activity, and at stake is the actual course of human lives, and therefore the quality of human interactions; philosophy of education is the heart and soul of school activity, and at stake is the actual course of children's lives and the quality of classroom interactions. To regard reflection upon philosophies as a useless frill is a philistinism of the worst kind; reflection is not only useful, it is crucial.

I conclude that since intelligent people insist on questioning, and since we wish teachers to be intelligent people, and since a teacher's attitude is of paramount practical import and is determined by that teacher's philosophy, philosophy of education courses as here conceived are essential within any teacher preparation program. It is the virtue of philosophy of education, not its crime, that it is ivory tower, out of the fray, for by reason of the 'distance' it affords, it gives perspective on aims and values in education which in turn issues in attitude, in a way of treating students and the world, and in a sense of informed personal purpose. Only if we wish to attract the unreflective to the teaching profession, and only if we wish teacher attitudes to be determined by chance upbringing or government decree, could we seriously contemplate eliminating courses in philosophy of education.

Notes

1. In making value questions primary, I am not attempting to demean epistemology (e.g. in curricula theory), aesthetics, or conceptual analysis. To begin with, I don't see how one can seriously tackle value questions without pushing into epistemology, aesthetics and conceptual clarity. But I am saying that in teacher training, under fiscal fire, the consideration of value questions must be considered essential, that which, when all else has yielded to pressure, must not be yielded.

2. A thumbnail sketch of Nietzsche's philosophy is bound to fail, such is the fecundity, and epigrammatic style, of his writing. My use of the coupling "power-creativity" (and "power-vitality") is my attempt to be concise without incurring severe distortion. Stressing one side of the coupling at the expense of the other will distort Nietzsche's position: stress power and Nietzsche quickly becomes a Darwinian monster and suitable support for Hitler; stress creativity and Nietzsche comes out as unrealistic about the realities of power and social pressures. Nietzsche was neither. The decisive thrust of Nietzsche is the creation of values: "But at some future time, a time stronger than our effete, self-doubting present, the true Redeemer will come, whose surging creativity will not let him rest..." (Nietzsche, 56, p. 229);"...the ripest fruit of that tree to be the sovereign individual, equal only to himself, all moral custom left far behind. This autonomous, more than moral individual (the terms 'autonomous' and 'moral' are mutually exclusive) has developed his own, independent, long-range will..." (Nietzsche, 56, p. 191); "Industry, modesty, benevolence, temperance are just so many hindrances to a sovereign disposition, great inventiveness, heroic purposiveness, noble being-for-oneself..." (Nietzsche, 67, p. 169). My sketch leans a little to the power side and to that extent fails. However, my purpose is not to give a scholarly and complete exegesis of Nietzschean philosophy; rather it is to show how philosophies such as these bear on education.

3. Cf. "The task of those who are for practical purposes rulers, leaders, employers, squires, and guides of the people, should be to take good care where they are going and whither they are leading. But in fact, the words 'ruler' and 'leader' are not applied to them; they are denied this style and title. The false dogma of equality, so flattering to the weak, results in practice in a chartered libertinism for the strong.

At no time in history has social elevation carried with it fewer obligations, or actual inequality proved more oppressive, than since the incorporation in positive law of an equality in principle bringing in its train the negation of all the duties that belong to station." (Bertrand de Jouvenal, 1962, p. 374)

References

De Jouvenal, B. *On Power*. Boston: Beacon Press, 1962.
Nietzsche, F. *Beyond Good and Evil*. New York: Random House, 1966. *The Will to Power*. New York: Random House, 67. *The Birth of Tragedy and the Geneology of Morals*. New York: Doubleday, 56.

Chapter 2

Summerhill Revisited

A. S. Neill insisted that the word "lazy" can never be correctly used of a child in a learning situation; rather one should say that the child is "uninterested" or "sick".

> Laziness doesn't exist. (Neill, p. 357)

> What is called laziness is either lack of interest or lack of health. (p. 59)

Most teachers and parents, and undoubtedly most if not all students, would totally disagree with Neill. Surely we all know what it is to be lazy in a learning situation, to make little or no effort at learning. How much credence then, if any, can we give to Neill's seemingly wild claim?

At the outset, let us be clear that the dispute centres on the correctness of the word "lazy" when applied to a young learner, not on the pedagogical appropriateness of the word. That is, if calling a child lazy causes him or her to give up and become resentful, then in a teaching-learning situation the term can be inappropriate. On the other hand, if calling a child lazy causes him or her to try harder and do better, then in a teaching-learning situation the term can be appropriate. But we are not concerned with the consequences of using the term "lazy", we are concerned only with whether or not "lazy" can be correctly used of a child in a learning situation.

If I say, "John, you are lazy when it comes to learning x", I strictly assume that John ought to be learning x. One does not appropriately call a person lazy for not studying poetry if one sees no call for him to be studying poetry, nor would one call a person lazy for sitting out in the sun all day, dozing, when one understands that the person is overworked and has been ordered to rest by his doctor. I also strictly assume that John is not learning x to the degree to which he could in fact be learning x. One does not appropriately call a person lazy for not reading poetry if he currently cannot owing to eye injury, nor does one call a brain-damaged child lazy for not keeping up with his peers in mathematics. Most importantly, in terming John lazy I am not merely describing his behaviour, rather I am blaming him. I blame him precisely because he could be learning x, ought to be learning x and is not learning x. Blaming is the main point of using the term "lazy".

If Neill insists that "lazy" can never be correctly applied to a child in a learning situation, he could be asserting either that there is nothing a child ought to learn, or that in fact the child could not be learning better, or both. This latter, both, is precisely Neill's position.

Neill does not accept that a child ought to learn anything. For Neill, young people have a right to play, a right ultimately warranted by health. Trying to push Neill into a fairly clear philosophical slot, we can say that he is holding on to a form of naturalism. Kittens are naturally playful and curious, and to lock them up would be wrong because it is denying a natural movement towards happiness. Children are naturally playful and curious, and to force them into schools where they become bored, anxious, or pressured is wrong because it is denying a natural movement towards happiness. This denial of happiness, moreover, is the fundamental root of ill-health, both individual and societal: pressured repressed children become neurotic, and unhappy children become resentful, hostile or obsequious.

> I ask what earthly good can come out of discussions about French or ancient history or what not when these subjects don't matter a jot compared to the larger question of life's natural fulfillment—of man's inner happiness. (p. 24)

> The aim of life is happiness. The evil of life is all that limits or destroys happiness. Happiness always means goodness; and unhappiness at its extreme limits means Jew-baiting, minority torture, or war. (p. 111)

> In all countries, capitalist, socialist, or communist, elaborate schools are built to educate the young. But all the wonderful labs and workshops do nothing to help John or Peter or Ivan surmount the emotional damage and the social evils bred by the pressure of the coercive quality of our civilization. (p. 28)

The 'ought to learn x' is thus at the root of educational evils since it licenses the teacher to pressure John to learn, to wield carrots and sticks, and licenses in John an acceptance of guilt feelings when he fails to meet teacher expectations. It also rationalizes for all an acceptance of dull and anxiety-ridden experiences.

Not only is pressure to learn, the 'ought', wrong, it is unnecessary, since happy, healthy children will learn all they need to learn. Readiness-motivation is the fundamental precondition of good learning. It cannot be compelled, since interest is spontaneous, and it need not be pursued, since it will arise naturally as a child interacts with the environment. If frustrated in pursuing his wishes, a child will naturally seek help. As he grows up, the responsibilities and opportunities of adult life will come into focus and he will respond to these natural pressures by learning what is needful. People learn most, most happily, when the desire is there, whether that desire be part and parcel of an instinct to play or whether it be part and parcel of a reasoned judgement that since I want x, I will have to learn y.

In sum, pressuring learning, for Neill, is wrong since it makes for unhappiness, and it is stupid since it is unnecessary.

> But true interest is the life force of the whole personality, and such interest is completely spontaneous....Though one can compel attention, one cannot compel interest. (p. 162)

> My view is that a child is innately wise and realistic. If left to himself without adult suggestion of any kind, he will develop as far as he is capable of developing. (p. 4)

> The whole idea of Summerhill is release: allowing the child to live out his natural interests. A school should make a child's life a game. I do not mean that the child should have a path of roses. Making it easy for the child is fatal to the child's character. But life itself presents so many difficulties that the artificial difficulties which we present to children are unnecessary.
> I believe that to impose anything by authority is wrong. The child should not do anything until he comes to the opinion—his own opinion—that it should be done. The curse of humanity is the external compulsion, whether it comes from the Pope or the state or the teacher or the parent. It is fascism in toto. (p. 114)

Furthermore, given the view that play and learning come naturally, Neill has to conclude, and does, that if a child in a learning situation is inactive (lazy) someone else is to blame since there is a very real sense in which the child cannot learn. Healthy young people are naturally curious, active, energetic. If a healthy child is bored or completely uninterested, his environment must be such that his natural energies and curiosities are being repressed.

Given a repressive environment and certain natural laws about the effects of repression of natural tendencies, a child cannot more actively pursue the learning of x. This "cannot" indicates not so much "is literally unable", as "the cards are stacked against him". To compel a child to learn that in which he has not the slightest interest is to stack the cards against his learning in the same way that to feed a person rotten meat, all the while insisting it is for his own good health, stacks the cards against his continuing to eat more and more rotten meat. No doubt he does have the mechanical ability to chew and swallow it, but the effects are so shattering on a system that naturally moves toward health, and so contrary to his own sense of well-being, that his rebellion and rejection are natural. So it is also with forced learning. To force learning on a child is to be responsible for that child's boredom and lack of interest, is to be blameworthy, is to be condemned. One should not chain up kittens and try to compel them to do tricks. Learning that comes naturally, by contrast, involves no feelings of repression and no painful upset.

Thus Neill holds that there is nothing a child ought to learn, and if he is not learning well there is a sense in which he cannot, so the blame for his inactivity lies elsewhere. Being unable, then, to blame the child, he must obviously reject the term "lazy" and must substitute a word that is non-accusatory and fairer to the facts—hence he uses either "sick" or "uninterested". Thus laziness doesn't exist.

Most radical critiques of education have centered around the rejection of the 'ought to learn x' and the absolute folly of trying to coerce learning on the uninterested. Who are we to push our values onto others? How dare we create anxiety and boredom in the name of education, create distaste for learning in the name of learning? It is characteristic of these critiques that they never talk of the lazy child; rather they dwell on authoritarian, insensitive schools. The following is typical.

> If he can just be kept out of school, he won't be taught that learning is dull, unpleasant work. He'll just assume it's what it is: the greatest pleasure in human life. There'll be no guilt and no fear. . . . School is a terrible thing to do to kids. It's cruel, unnatural, unnecessary. . . . It [school] warps your expectations so that you'll see the outside world like the school and then you'll tend to make your world that way. You'll be trained to see learning as hard and painful. And you'll go out and perpetuate a world in which those conditions exist. You know, you have to teach any organism how to be unhappy. And the human being is the only organism that has learned unhappiness—except maybe some of his has

spilled over onto his dog. I must insist that schools as they now exist are well designed to produce unhappiness and little else. (Sullivan, quoted in Leonard, pp. 104–106)

The world is filled with wrongs—war, disease, famine, racial degradation and all the slaveries man has invented for his own kind. But none is more deep or more poignant than the systematic destruction of the human spirit that, all too often, is the hidden function of every school. (Leonard, p. 110)

For Neill and fellow travellers, given Neill's view of man and ethics, it would indeed be incorrect to use the term "lazy" of a child in a learning situation. But I wish to claim that they are wrong, and in being wrong they have done serious disservice to our schools.

If John has a certain goal in mind then it is perfectly legitimate to say that he ought to do what is necessary to achieve it. If he wants to be a doctor and refuses to make any efforts to learn in school, and if it is reasonably certain that unless he does well in school he will never be accepted for medical training, it seems correct to call him lazy. We thus blame him for his inactivity because he could be learning but isn't, and because he ought to be learning given the goal he has chosen. This "ought" is not a clear case of a moral ought, and hence is interchangeable with the less urgent "should". We are not so much righteously condemning his inactivity as we are being exasperated by it; it is not so much the morality of the student which is in question as his rationality or common sense.

But this example does not defeat Neill's claim that laziness does not exist, because in ordinary circumstances it is inconceivable. If John really wants to become a doctor, and if it is clear one is required to have certain transcripts, then John will do what is necessary. His failure to do what is necessary would simply indicate that the desire was little more than a whim or fancy. The accusations of laziness are typically associated with the unmotivated student, the one who seems to have no aims at all.

Since all individuals eventually have to take their place in the world, earn a living, or at least fill up the time one way or another, we might well say that all children, motivated or otherwise, need a modicum of skills and abilities, and therefore ought to (should) learn them. But Neill can quickly dismiss this argument. For Neill, the important thing is that the child will learn when he feels the need or desire to, and to introduce the notion of ought, with its inevitable baggage of pressures, is to misconceive and distort the whole business of learning. Instead of obliterating the world of play and genuine interest under the banner "Preparation for Adulthood", we must let the child live out his play life, let him pursue what he actually does find interesting, and then we can be sure that this happy and self-confident youth will be able to tackle well any tasks that might fall his way in adulthood. That is, play and happiness are a better preparation for work than work is. This is a prediction, so only a future can declare it false. However, the evidence of Neill's own school favours the prediction. Furthermore, given the speed of change, it becomes harder to specify what modicum of skills and abilities will be required, and Neill's claim regarding self-confident youth makes intuitive good sense. All the above notwithstanding, I wish to claim that one can correctly term the inactive, unmotivated child in school lazy.

My argument is straightforward. Young people ought to work hard in schools because compulsory, universal education is a singular social achievement. Schools are, in the main, staffed and directed by humane people intent on equipping a child for a rich adult life, rich in abilities, appreciations, and, hopefully, job opportunities. Furthermore, the education system is funded by tax monies, which is to say that waitresses, bus drivers, and construction workers, amongst many others, pay for it. Furthermore, the vast majority of parents want children to benefit from school.

Surely at the heart of morality is the consideration of others. If for no other reason, out of consideration for the work and wishes of adults, children ought to take full advantage of schools designed to benefit them. Say what you will about interest, creativity, freedom to learn, and indoctrination, a root question is whether it is only adults who have duties to children or whether children also have duties to adults. If you reject the notion that children have duties to adults, then certainly the unmotivated inactive child cannot correctly be described as lazy, since he cannot be blamed unless one argues he has obligations to his own self-development. But if you accept the notion, then it would seem that one can correctly call the unmotivated inactive child lazy for the very good reason that he owes it to others not to waste what they have gone to some lengths to provide.

Furthermore, given intelligent and half-decent teaching, students can learn. It only requires effort. And whether or not I make an effort is up to me. The assumption involved is that choice is not an illusion; I am not a puppet of genes-cum-stimuli having to wait to be correctly jerked so that I can move appropriately. Moreover mathematics, history, geography, or whatever, is nothing like rotten meat, and will only upset a sense of well-being if the person has learned to feel no obligations.

Neill would quickly retort that whilst students have duties to adults, trying hard in school is not one of them. Freedom is not licence, and children must respect the rights of others, including adults; but learning, Neill insisted, is a private matter, and hence is nobody else's business or concern.

> In our educational policy as a nation, we refuse to let live. We persuade through fear. But there is a great difference between compelling a child to cease throwing stones and compelling him to learn Latin. Throwing stones involves others; but learning Latin involves only the boy. The community has the right to restrain the antisocial boy because he is interfering with the rights of others; but the community has no right to compel a boy to learn Latin—for learning Latin is a matter for the individual. Forcing a child to learn is on a par with forcing a man to adopt a religion by act of Parliament. And it is equally foolish. (p. 115)

> Children should be free to question the rules of etiquette, for eating peas with a knife is a personal thing. They should not be free to question what might be called social manners. If a child enters our drawing room with muddy boots, we shout at him, for the drawing room belongs to adults, and the adults have the right to decree what and who shall enter and what and who shall not. (p. 193)

But how can one term learning a private matter when parents worry about whether their children are learning? When society at large puts up huge sums of money for the building and maintaining of a universal school system? When the majority of adults want a compulsory school system? When the future of our society is in the hands of the young? Learning is not a private matter, it is a public matter; whether my child learns is far more important than whether he comes into my living room with dirty boots. Children do have duties to adults, and to make the most of the opportunities afforded by schools is surely one of them.

Critics will be quick, however, and correct, to state that one can concede that education is a public matter, that students are not puppets, and that students have duties to adults, and still reject the assertion that making the most of schools is one of these duties. They will argue that all of the foregoing is largely an obfuscation, a muddying of the basic issue, which is that our society is essentially immoral, schools are a major agency of socialization, therefore schools are immoral, therefore students have no duty to make the most of schools (which is, in effect, to support them) no matter how many people fund them or believe in them; mathematics may not be like rotten meat but, nevertheless, the open curriculum and the teaching of it can be boring and destructive of enthusiasm and creativity, and the hidden curriculum, feeding a competitive society with suitably self-seeking insensitive-to-inequality youth, is as corrupting as it is insidious. In short, critics will insist that far from being a singular social achievement, schooling is a powerful instrument of immorality. This, after all, was the major thrust of Neill, though he would probably prefer the word "sick" to "immoral".

To this I must reply that any society is in a sense immoral; schools are a major agency of socialization; all schools are tainted by social immorality; our schools nevertheless are indeed a singular social achievement, and our students do have the obligation to make the most of them.

All societies are inevitably immoral if by morality we refer to justice, equality, caring, and such-like. It will always be the case that some people have more power than others. Man's ability to care will always be limited by value clash and by his own emotional resources. Moreover, it will always be the case that moral conceptions will be impossible to pin down in clear, precise and agreed fashion; moral notions are essentially contestable.[1] Thus the charge of immorality can, and probably will, be continually and plausibly made.

Childhood is inevitably socialization; schooling is clearly socialization. Hidden curricula are everywhere and inevitable; the medium can't help but be the message/massage. Arguments, then, based on the immorality of society and its agents of socialization, with their open and hidden curricula, are trivial at least in the sense that the same arguments could be used against any society. But clearly, some societies are morally better than others; some societies are openly brutal whilst others make serious attempts to aid the weak ("morality" does have a central core meaning which typically permits meaningful discussion and debate, the essential contestability of moral concepts notwithstanding). How, then, should we make the moral distinction?

A society and its institutions should be judged essentially by how possible it is for morally-convinced persons, despite their often being at odds with one another (and, in my view, always with themselves[2]), to engage in the struggle for a better society, and by how much the society has moved in a moral direction as compared with its own past and with the states of affairs in other societies. The main indicators of the very possibility of moral struggle are free media (that is, no government censorship of press, T.V., radio and such), laws granting freedom of speech, assembly, religion and unionization, a government elected by the people and a free and universal school system where questions of fact and value are vigorously and humanely pursued.

The evils of our society have been overplayed by such as Neill. The West and its schools are in a sense immoral, yet when judged by the criteria outlined above, they are indeed good. Western society, with its strong democratic freedoms and lively moral tradition, is no mean achievement; its critics rarely attempt to leave. Western schooling is a singular social achievement: our schools are better than most and better than heretofore; every child has the right to personal development through formal education. The possibility of struggle toward a better social form is firmly in place.

The evils of forced learning have been overplayed. If interest is spontaneous then it can occur anywhere, including a school classroom. The belief that children will develop to their fullest potential without adult suggestion of any kind is not demonstrable and seems particularly foolish. Learning is not merely a private matter, and a little boredom in a worthwhile cause does nobody any harm.

Happiness has been overplayed; it is more complex than Neill allows. There is happiness, for example, in fulfilling one's obligations.

I therefore conclude that students who are not making the most of our schools are indeed lazy; the older the child, the more appropriate this accusation is. Poor schools may be a consequence of poor teaching, but may also be a consequence of poor learning. School is hurt by lazy teachers who feel no obligation to their students, but is equally hurt by lazy students who feel no obligation to their society. Automatically blaming teachers or the school system for educational failures does them a serious disservice.

Notes

1. Is it caring to give a beggar ten dollars, or is it condescending? Is it fair that lawyers are paid more than bus drivers? Are persons equally worthy of respect?

Cf. "The concepts of the moral and political are both what has been called 'essentially contestable'. This means, among other things, both that the questions of where the proper boundaries are to be drawn between the moral and non-moral, between the political and the non-political, raise issues that are themselves of moral or political significance, and that there may be real and indissoluble conflicts of moral or political values." A. Montefiore,

"Philosophy and Moral (and Political) Education", *Journal of Philosophy of Education*, Vol. 13, 79.

2. I hold moral notions to be self-contradictory in a Marxian sense of "contradictory". The only thesis I know which more or less states this and fully explains it, is J.-P. Sartre, *Being and Nothingness*, wherein values such as goodness are reflections of an impossible union of being-in-itself and being-for-itself, a union which necessarily haunts being-for-itself. See also my chapters 4, 9 and 10.

Cf. "Consider first—the question of whether there can occur irreducible conflicts of moral values or obligations, conflicts of which there may be no morally acceptable resolution. What is at stake here is not the question of relations between different and incomparable moral outlooks held by different individuals or societies, but rather that of whether one and the same point of view can or must allow for the possibility of such clashes. This question goes pretty deep." A. Montefiore, op. cit.

References

Leonard, G. *Education and Ecstasy*. N. York: Dell Publishing, 1968.
Neill, A. S. *Summerhill*. N. York: Hart Publishing, 1960.

Chapter 3

The Absurd Teacher

Beginning to think is beginning to be undermined.
(Camus, p. 4)

In Greek legend, Sisyphus was condemned by the gods to rolling a stone to the top of a mountain, seeing it roll back down again, returning to roll it up again, and doing this for ever: "... that unspeakable penalty in which the whole being is exerted toward accomplishing nothing." (p. 89) Sisyphus was, for Camus, a graphic illustration of the absurd man, of the man Camus' reflecting on life led him to admire.

Reflecting on life, Camus found that he wished to understand that of which he was a part; he wanted to know the point, and rules, of life.

> I see many people die because they judge that life is not worth living. I see others paradoxically getting killed for ideas or illusions that give them a reason for living (what is called a reason for living is also an excellent reason for dying). I therefore conclude that the meaning of life is the most urgent of questions. (p. 3)

It became transparently clear to Camus, at the time of writing anyway, that not only did he not know the meaning of life, but that neither he nor anyone else had any conceivable hope of ever knowing. Why there is something rather than nothing is clearly beyond the grasp of reason; we cannot know the origin of all things (though we can make defensible guesses). It seems equally clear that nobody can know, though we can always guess, the ultimate destiny, or destination, of all things. And to whom do we go in order to discover the values we ought to live by? And how does he or she know? We are evidently caught up in a situation where the beginning, the end, and how one ought to live in the present, is beyond the knowing of man. Logic ends up in paradox, science ends up in paradigm and the uncertainty principle: reason has its limits. The fact that the society we grow up in has its own brand of order and purpose, and of "ought", can hardly be taken as a definitive answer to the larger questions, though we may well take comfort from the answers it proffers.

To be alive then and to reflect on this as Camus did, is like waking up on a bus and discovering that nobody knows where it came from, where it ought to be heading, or how they ought to operate within the bus. The bus is orderly and moving in a certain direction, for a bus (that is, cultural) game has been historically imposed and is being imposed, but whether the game is the one the passengers ought to be playing, no one can know. And looking around the bus, Camus sees many instances of pain, suffering and death. He is seared, estranged, by the uselessness of suffering and by the evident lack of profound meaning, of high purpose. Longing to understand, and unable to, Camus senses the universe as hostile. Radically alienated, afloat on a sea of incomprehensibility without a star to steer by, he clings desperately to his own lucidity and to the absurdity it reveals: the absurdity of rational man locked into an irrational, that is, incomprehensible, situation.

> . . . in a universe suddenly divested of illusions and lights, man feels an alien, a stranger. His exile is without remedy since he is deprived of the memory of a lost home or the hope of a promised land. (p. 5)

> I said that the world is absurd, but I was too hasty. This world in itself is not reasonable, that is all that can be said. But what is absurd is the confrontation of this irrational and the wild longing for clarity whose call echoes in the human heart. The absurd depends as much on man as on the world. For the moment it is all that links them together. It binds them one to the other as only hatred can weld two creatures together. This is all I can discern clearly in this measureless universe where my adventure takes place. Let us pause here. If I hold to be true that absurdity that determines my relationship with life, if I become thoroughly imbued with the sentiment that seizes me in the face of the world's scenes, with that lucidity imposed on me by the pursuit of a science, I must sacrifice everything to these certainties and I must see them squarely to be able to maintain them. Above all, I must adapt my behaviour to them and pursue them in all their consequences. I am speaking here of decency. (p. 16)

Certain of the absurd, Camus is nevertheless well aware of the keys which liberate one from it. One key is the leap of faith. Religion, ideologies, and some philosophies will answer questions regarding the purpose of life, will declare the true values and the right ethic, and some will even tell you why there is something rather than nothing and how the whole show will end up. They give life a profound meaning, a high purpose, and thus give birth to the evangelical, the missionary, the revolutionary. But Camus has made a fateful decision: he prefers lucidity, that is, he will stick to what he knows. "Hence, what he demands of himself is to live solely with what he knows, to accommodate himself to what is, and to bring in nothing that is not certain." (p. 39) It is not that the religions, ideologies, and philosophies are false, but rather that we can not know that they are true. A second key is the plunge into the everyday, the submersion of oneself in the current bus game. "In The Castle the surrender to the everyday becomes an ethic." (p. 98) The everyday is replete with manifold meanings and understandings—getting to work, watching your kids grow up, understanding what is going on when it thunders and lightens, understanding why certain legislation was passed, and so on. The everyday is meaningful and has its attendant pleasures. By immersing ourselves in it, we push aside the question of profound meaning, of high purpose, of understanding why there is something rather than nothing; we play to the hilt the cultural game, the rules and point of which we were inducted into.

Thus one key gives you profound meaning and purpose, an understanding of the 'whole', whilst the other key gives you manifold meanings, purposes, and understandings such that not only are the larger questions shut out but, if raised, they strike one as incongruous, stupid, absurd. Camus, in full consciousness, rejects both the leap of faith and the plunge into the everyday. He is trying to base his living on the truth, on what an insistent demand for lucidity brings forth—and to that extent at least, he embodies the traditional quest of philosophy.

Standing only on lucidity, shedding his world of leaps and plunges, Camus finds himself radically innocent. "He feels innocent. To tell the truth that is all he feels—his irreparable innocence." (p. 39) The heavy ethical codes typically spawned by religions, ideologies, and philosophies, and the societal rules taken so seriously, have disappeared along with the rejection of the leap and the plunge. Camus can feel no guilt, neither can he feel virtue. All is given, nothing is explained, nothing prescribed from beyond men. This does not mean that Camus will scoff at societal rules, for to do so would be silly—the bus needs a game. And although he can feel no guilt, he can feel regret.

> There is but one moral code that the absurd man can accept, the one that is not separated from God: the one that is

dictated. But it so happens that he lives outside that God. As for the others (I mean also immoralism) the absurd man sees nothing in them but justifications and he has nothing to justify. I start here from the principle of his innocence. That innocence is to be feared. "Everything is permitted," exclaims Ivan Karamazov. That, too, smacks of the absurd. But on condition that it not be taken in the vulgar sense. I don't know whether or not it has been sufficiently pointed out that it is not an outburst of relief or of joy, but rather a bitter acknowledgement of fact. The certainty of a God giving a meaning to life far surpasses in attractiveness the ability to behave badly with impunity. The choice would not be hard to make. But there is no choice, and that is where the bitterness comes in. The absurd does not liberate; it binds. It does not authorize all actions. "Everything is permitted" does not mean that nothing is forbidden. The absurd merely confers an equivalence on the consequences of those actions. It does not recommend crime, for this would be childish, but it restores to remorse its futility. Likewise, if all experiences are indifferent, that of duty is as legitimate as any other. One can be virtuous through a whim.

All systems of morality are based on the idea that an action has consequences that legitimize or cancel it. A mind imbued with the absurd merely judges that those consequences must be considered calmly. It is ready to pay up. In other words, there may be responsible persons, but there are no guilty ones, in its opinion. (p. 49ff.)*

Deeply alienated, radically innocent, the absurd man defies the surrounding darkness by living, by consciously rolling the stone day after day until he falls victim to the final, inscrutable incomprehensible. Camus rages at the night. Death and suffering are never explained away; the desire to understand, always thwarted, is as strong as ever. But he defiantly rolls his rock. Freed from the demanding ethics of quality, with their attendant loads of virtue and guilt, freed from the weight of a demanding future (in the sense that he does not know he will have a tomorrow, and in the sense that his life style is not to be dictated by promised heavens, classless societies, the Oneness of Being, or whatever), freed from the dictates of a profound meaning-purpose of life, consciousness is liberated into a heightened awareness of the present.

Completely turned toward death (taken here as the most obvious absurdity), the absurd man feels released from everything outside that passionate attention crystallizing in him. He enjoys a freedom with regard to common rules. . . .

---

*I quote this at length since to understand this passage is to understand the heart of Camus' thinking.

> The return to consciousness, the escape from the everyday
> sleep represent the first steps of absurd freedom. (pp. 43, 44)

Despite all the futility, all the straining, Sisyphus rolls the rock with his own hands. He feels the texture of the rock and the tension exerted on him by the slope. He sees the sky, the vast blueness, the wisps of white, the subtle shades of colour on the horizon. He is sensitively conscious of the teeming diversity around him. He feels, dramatically, his own existing—and the beauty, and sense of wonder, overwhelm him. "One must imagine Sisyphus happy." (p. 91)

The absurd teacher is one who sees his condition clearly, who rails against the incomprehensibility, and who dwells heavily in the present. Not that he never thinks of tomorrow, or next year, for that would be silly. But the present is where he finds his wealth: John's smile, Mary's face, the clamour of kids, the everyday drama as seen by one who has seized awareness. This sensitivity to people and things in the present creates a warmish atmosphere in the class. His sense of wonder counters his sense of the tragic, and what eventuates in his teaching is a quiet enthusiasm, an openness and amazement toward the natural world.

> Likewise, the absurd man, when he contemplates his tor-
> ment, silences all the idols. In the universe suddenly restored
> to its silence, the myriad wondering little voices of the earth
> rise up. Unconscious, secret calls, invitations from all the
> faces, they are the necessary reverse and price of victory.
> There is no sun without shadow, and it is essential to know
> the night...(p. 91)

The absurd teacher, quiet, aware, finds it very hard to be aggressive and violent, for he has no high calling, no profound meaning, no righteous cause. On the other hand, he is not stupid about the need for social order, nor will he sit back if lucidity, awareness, and beauty are threatened, for these are his values. Students quickly become aware that his tolerance has limits, that he does have values, but they notice he gets no pleasure from victory. Similarly, the absurd teacher does get involved in the day-to-day disputes of the school; he understands and accepts that one should not flee the concerns of the day. But his heart is not in it. Perpetual struggle to impose or gain power in some form or other may be necessary but it is ignoble; it is a bore.

> The secret I am seeking lies hidden in a valley full of olive
> trees, under the grass and the cold violets, around an old
> house that smells of wood smoke. For more than twenty

years I rambled over that valley and others resembling it, I questioned mute goat-herds, I knocked at the door of deserted ruins. Occasionally, at the moment of the first star in the still bright sky, under a shower of shimmering light, I thought I knew. I did know, in truth. I still know, perhaps. But no one wants any of this secret; I don't want any myself, doubtless; and I cannot stand apart from my people. I live in my family, which thinks it rules over rich and hideous cities built of stones and mists. Day and night it speaks up, and everything bows before it, which bows before nothing: it is deaf to all secrets. Its power that carries me bores me, nevertheless, and on occasion its shouts weary me. But its misfortune is mine, and we are of the same blood. A cripple, likewise, an accomplice and noisy, have I not shouted among the stones? Consequently, I strive to forget, I walk in our cities of iron and fire, I smile bravely at the night, I hail the storms, I shall be faithful. I have forgotten, in truth: active and deaf, henceforth. But perhaps someday, when we are ready to die of exhaustion and ignorance, I shall be able to disown our garish tombs and go and stretch out in the valley, under the same light, and learn for the last time what I know. (p. 145)

Unwilling to flee the concerns of the day, the absurd teacher inevitably becomes involved in the lurching course of educational bandwagons: from authority to freedom, from freedom to authority, from choice to basics, from basics to choice, from kindness to pressure, from pressure to kindness, from self-motivation to group dynamics, from group dynamics to self-motivation, from the unquantifiable to behavioural objectives, from behavioural objectives to the unquantifiable, from relationships to technology, from technology to relationships. . . . Imbued as he is with a sense of wonder, and having a very clear notion of the limits of reason, the absurd teacher sees the frantic shifts as essentially trivial, as the pursuit of clear answers to muddy questions. It is the lurching of the bus as different people struggle for the wheel. It is history. But behind history is being, behind the future is the present, and behind causes are the sky and faces. The absurd teacher does not flee the struggles of his time, but neither does he find therein his riches.

> . . .man cannot do without beauty, and this is what our era pretends to want to disregard. It steels itself to attain the absolute and authority; it wants to transfigure the world before having exhausted it, to set it to rights before having understood it. (p. 137)

The absurd teacher understands monotony and drudgery, the daily grind, the meaninglessness of it all in the time span of the universe—this is life, not to be fled from, to be wept over, or to be dressed up into something better. He willingly, in full consciousness, chooses the teacher's lot, the pushing of that particular rock. Lucidity, awareness, and beauty will dominate and pervade his view, and practice, of education. The absurd man delights in reason, his awareness of its limits notwithstanding. Teaching mathematics, science, literature, social studies, and such, is to the absurd man as good a use of time as any. And the absurd teacher, being sensible, understands the need to get a job. He neither glamorizes nor blackens what is. He sees the joys and the sorrows, the point and the meaninglessness, the ecstasy and the tedium, and accepts all within the arc of his decision to live.

Haunted, then, by ignorance, surrounded by the incomprehensible, seared by suffering and death, bewitched by sky, water, faces, amazed at his own existing, the absurd teacher silences the strident voices of gods and begins to hear the quiet, myriad voices of this world. He is not trying to be better, only consistent.

> Admission of ignorance, rejection of fanaticism, the limits of
> the world and of man, the beloved face, and finally beauty—
> this is where we shall be on the side of the Greeks. (p. 138)

References

Camus, A. *The Myth of Sisyphus and Other Essays*. N. York: Vintage Books, 1955.

Chapter 4

A Critique of Moral Education in Schools

The importance of moral education seems obvious. Many contend that only a genuine moral sensitivity will prevent social conflagration, local and global: with limited resources, disproportionately shared, mankind must learn to co-operate if it is to survive in any decent fashion; mankind must eschew violence and embrace social justice and caring, or fail. Morality is the difference between community and jungle: morality tempers power, insisting on higher values of love and justice. It also appears that individuals need a sense of value, of ideals, of high purpose, of meaning. The affluent West is haunted by a sense of ennui, meaninglessness, ephemeral rancour. Morality, many contend, is the very essence of man—to be immoral or amoral is to be, in some sense or other, deeply warped and disfigured, to be less than human. Thus many insist that inasmuch and insofar as schools avoid direct moral education they are dehumanized and dehumanizing, disfiguring children and ultimately destructive of any decent social living.

It is not my wish to deny the importance of morality. It is clear that moral conceptions are man's highest ideals, shaping societies and giving individuals a sense of profound worth and right direction; the quality of life, for individual and society, in the final analysis rests upon man's moral ideals. Nor do I wish to contend that schools should not indulge in direct moral education since they cannot prove their particular conception of morality to be right. This latter contention is not a problem to be lightly tossed aside, but pushed to its limits it seems to imply that we should not influence the values of anyone else, especially children. Schools *do* influence the values of children, so responsible adults must consider to what specific extent, in what specific direction, and specifically how, schools will morally educate. Thus I applaud current concerns with moral education in schools. But I wish to point out the price of moral education in North American schools, given what I take to be a typical conception of "moral". I believe the price to be heavy.

By "morality" I henceforth essentially refer to any teaching that centres on notions that we ought to care for and about others and hence, that we should be honest in our dealings with people and should be actively concerned about social justice. Care, honesty, social justice—these seem to be the heart of morality, but in any case they constitute the heart of the morality I am here talking about. If you have a conception of morality that eliminates or downplays these ideals, I am surprised but anyway, I am simply not talking to your version. By "moral education" I essentially refer to the advancing of these ideals in schools, regardless of means or degrees of directness. What then could be the heavy price of advancing these ideals in our schools today, ideals that appear to be so badly needed and so intrinsically worthwhile?

If we imbue our youth with moral ideals and sensitivities, and then release them into a competitive society, we are essentially sending them out to a battlefield innocent, unprotected and unarmed. Just to get and keep a decent job one usually has to lie a little, or a lot, one needs to be able to manipulate those in power via friends, rhetoric or whatever, and one needs a powerful union or professional association which will use its muscle to exact good rewards for its members. In short, one needs power and a certain ruthlessness in using it. In business the profit motive is supreme and companies constantly seek to expand their power base, that is, their dominance in a certain market. In democratic government there is perpetual jockeying for power; the first rule of government is to retain power. And business, government, unions and individuals, all understand the fundamental importance of public relations and advertising. The politician relies heavily on rhetoric, on posturing, on image-making—true motives and strategic deals remain hidden. The businessman relies heavily on advertising—the art of the half-truth, the science of concealing what you want hidden and making prominent what will appeal. "Selling" is what North American life is all about. To be straightforwardly honest in a competitive society is to be naive—you don't show your hand, or not until you have won. One must learn to be "professional". Thus by power, achieved largely by manipulation which nearly always embodies less than honest dealings with people, winners, and therefore losers, emerge. Hospital orderlies earn $15,000 a year, plumbers earn $35,000 a year, while sharp wheeler dealers and drug pushers acquire fortunes. Lawyers, the social embodiment of justice, have so fixed fee schedules that they are very high on the income scale. Athletes and entertainers earn hundreds of thousands of dollars while a hardworking secretary is paid peanuts. Some struggle along on minimum wage while others seek to invest massive cash surpluses as profitably as they can. Half the world starves while the other half diets. . . . Honesty, justice and caring? You've got to be joking.

Worst of all, all this goes on bathed in the rhetoric of morality. Watergate and "God bless America"; hospital orderlies and "The Just Society"; all wage claims and all profits are always justified as "just" or "in the best interest of society" or "within our rights" or somesuch. . . . Consider the following newspaper report:

> An organizer for the Ontario Secondary School Teachers Federation told a meeting of Toronto area student leaders last night at Ryerson College that only political power could guarantee them what they want. . . . In addition to "being seen to represent your constituency", Mr. Geiger advised the students "to act with integrity—apparent integrity—which doesn't mean your tactics can't be sneaky—all political parties, governments and pressure groups use sneaky tactics—but you must maintain an aura of dignity."

The young moral person emerging into such a society, leaving the protection of home and school, can only recoil with horror. The societal rhetoric and the reality are at complete odds. Their society is hypocritical; their society is immoral. Power is all, principles are only for publication; power is the end and posturing, packaging, promotion and pressure are the means. The quick answer, the smart move, the right contacts, the right piece of paper, money in the right place, compromise, keeping one's nose clean until one has attained power—this is how our society works. Caring, honesty and social justice—little but fine words to cover up a ruthless and unfair social system.

The young moral person may react with massive anger. He pounds his fists against the bars of his helplessness—the power is in the hands of others, of those who are thriving on the system. His anger, fuelled by moral horror, knows no bounds. To change things one needs power, one must attain power. Soon the moralist is manipulating, half-truthing, pressuring, acquiring contacts or guns. So he soils his own hands with the dirt he despises in others. So his psychic unity is shattered; guilt, contradiction and loss of value contort a once-assured consciousness. The innocent, seeking an innocent society, has become guilty. The caring person, seeking a caring society, hurts people, many of them innocent bystanders. Worse still, the caring person must learn to cease to care inasmuch as care weakens, and one must be strong in the face of the forces of evil.

> For violence and hatred dry up the heart itself; the long fight for justice exhausts the love that nevertheless gave birth to it. In the clamour in which we live, love is impossible and justice does not suffice. (Camus, p. 144)

Or the young moral person may react by copping out. The horrors of power and profit and privilege, the deceit of packaging and posturing, are too much and his powerlessness too clear. So he cops out into a commune, rationalizes his way into living on unemployment or parental monies, or whatever. But by so doing he gives up on society, that is, on people. Others can struggle for social justice, he will live 'innocently'. In fact, he becomes part of a privileged elite, escaping the general struggle. Since he needs money, and since it must come from the system he despises so much, he in fact feeds off the spoils of injustice. Thus he serves injustice and noncaring. He is not innocent at all, and he knows it. His morality pushes him to flee and then condemns him for so doing. His mind can know no rest, his guilt and contradictions can yield no peace.

Or the young moral person may attempt to be "realistic". Competitive society has spawned many benefits. One must take one's place and by holding firm, in the main, to one's moral principles, one will, with others, gradually improve society. The framework of democracy encourages and heartens such a view. So you seek a job, you seek to support your family. You resist the violent excesses of the radical moralist, and you have not copped out. You are doing what you reasonably, all things considered, can. But you do have to compromise. Time and daily pressures slowly erode moral sensibilities, especially in times of stress—for example, times of inflation and insecure employment. It becomes increasingly clear, over the years, that you are as selfish as the next man. One day you wake up and face the terrifying truth that your pleas for social justice, truth and caring for others no longer reflect a real moral concern at all—your call for justice is born not out of love of the poor but out of jealousy of the rich, your call for truth not out of respect for people but out of anger at having been conned so often, and your call for caring not out of moral sensitivity but out of mere habit. The system has slowly but surely bought you off. You are in fact the very oil and cogs of the system. You have the power, having done what was required, but you have lost the values. Your guilt and sense of loss know no end. You have not ceased to believe in your moral values but you have lived their denial: you are the embodiment of hypocrisy, and have lost all grounding to declare on moral issues; your mind adheres to moral values but you no longer feel for them. It is all words and no soul. Morality led you to enter and improve the system and now condemns you for compromise.

In essence, the moral person is caught and mercilessly torn by the tension between real and ideal. Between power and principle there can be no peace. Yet principle demands power in order that it be made effective in the real world. Driven by principle to acquire power, the moral person both compromises and contravenes principle. So he is guilty. A guilty innocent. A quiet desperation, a sense of deep loss of value, a corrosive disquiet, attend this tragic plight of moral man. Let us weakly call it "alienation".

> In the light from conflagrations the world had suddenly shown its wrinkles and its wounds, old and new. It had aged all at once, and we with it. . . . No love without a little innocence. Where was the innocence? Empires were tumbling down; nations and men were tearing at one another's throats; our hands were soiled. Originally innocent without knowing it, we were now guilty without meaning to be: the mystery was increasing with our knowledge. This is why, O mockery, we were concerned with morality. Weak and disabled I was dreaming of virtue! (Camus, p. 141)

Exacerbating this deep alienation is the haunting suspicion that morality is essentially unreasonable, is foolish. For example, the call to caring, honesty and social justice typically assumes that man is worthy and capable of these, that man is basically good. This optimistic view of man is not easy to sustain—all of human history argues against it. The overwhelming evidence is not that man is essentially bad but rather that man is capable of almost anything— from extreme brutality to exquisite gentleness. The moral person, being basically optimistic of man, basically trusting, will naturally blame the environment for man's shortcomings. Not only does he have to, since what else can he blame, but it fits in with his call to reform society, to make society moral. However, since greed and violence flourish, this optimism is more and more put to the test. Consider the following newspaper account:

> Women wept and men buried their faces in their hands as Isaacs' 16-year-old brother, Billy, told of a reign of terror culminating in the shooting of five men and the rape-slaying of a wife.

Billy said his brother (Carl Isaacs, 19), and a halfbrother, Wayne Carl Coleman, 26, and George Dungee, 36, picked him up near Baltimore, Md., after they escaped from a Maryland prison farm last spring.

They travelled through Pennsylvania, West Virginia, the Carolinas and Florida before stopping at the house trailer of Jerry Alday, 35, to look for "money, guns, clothes, anything like that we could use." Billy said Jerry Alday and his father, Ned, 62, returned to the trailer and were taken to separate bedrooms and shot in the head as they lay face down on the beds.

When Ned's youngest son, Jimmy, 25, came home, he also was executed. "Carl came out of the bedroom laughing," Billy said. He said, "That damn bastard begged for mercy."

The men were holding Jerry's wife, Mary, 24, when the last two men came in. They were Ned's brother, Aubrey, 57, and his third son, Chester, 32. Both were murdered in cold blood. Billy said he left the trailer to help Coleman load their loot. When he looked inside he saw his brother raping Mary.

"I told Wayne that Carl was in there messing around with Mary Alday," he said. "Then Wayne went in and raped her."

The men then tied, gagged and blindfolded her, piled her into her own car and drove her to a wooded area. There, Billy said, she was dragged from the car and raped and beaten by his brother.

Billy said Carl gave Coleman a pistol and told him to kill the woman but Dungee said, "What about me? It's my turn." Dungee took the pistol, dragged her into the woods, raped her and shot her in the head and back.

The moralist finds it hard to believe that violence can be naturally enjoyable. Since, in the final analysis, one cannot demarcate "natural" from "learned", since all are subject to influences, the moralist's optimism is safe. Moreover the moralist's position rests upon a future state—a promise that if only social conditions were rearranged, men would be basically fair, honest and loving, a promise that love will beget love, trust will beget trust. Only time can prove a promise. As the promise fails to materialize, you simply blame current conditions and continue to promise a bright future for mankind once society changes its values and ways of operating. Thus your position is as irrefutable as it is unsubstantiated. But given daily contact with greedy, manipulating, violent people and institutions, and given a growing awareness that you are less than innocent yourself, reason demands that the assumption of man's worth be viewed critically. Perhaps man is essentially crummy. Perhaps one should love the loving and spit on the rest. Perhaps one should be honest with those one likes and respects, and deceive and use the rest. Perhaps some people deserve more, others less, and others nothing. In other words, principles which involve a call to general love, honesty and justice are foolishly non-discriminating. Perhaps morality is essentially stupid. Reason is suspect of morality. Morality and faith sustain each other, but reason has its doubts.

Morality also finds itself hapless when it bumps up against limits imposed by reality. Caring and social justice demand more or less equal sharing of wealth—one is immediately faced with what might be called the logic of money. Give food to starving countries and you lower the price of food and so discourage local farming. One man with ten million dollars can start an enterprise which will enable ten thousand employees to support their families well for decades. Share ten million dollars among ten million people and each can buy a coffee. Moral rhetoric is cheap. General Motors has done more, it can be argued, for real people than all the idealistic words ever aired—you cannot feed your children words. Lifeboat theories, economics in general, the inevitability of decision makers in any society and therefore the inevitability of power elites, that life is the need and/or desire for resources and that these are not infinite and hence conflicts arise, that there are psychological limits to caring and that one cannot choose to genuinely care, all this bewilders the moral person. It seems that to effect justice one must implement injustice, to benefit the poor, really, one needs the rich. The weak need the strong. Consider the following newspaper report:

> Hal Banks as SIU chieftain behaved and spent in flamboyant fashion. His expense accounts were enormous and literally unchecked. He holidayed in grand style, his expenses and those of his mistresses paid out of union funds. He drove a massive, white Cadillac. His entertainments for those on his own level in union affairs and politics were Rabelaisian. Justice Norris in his SIU inquiry picked apart much of this behaviour as improper or illegal. After his report and as the government moved to instal a trusteeship, the SIU mounted a major lobby campaign, its centrepiece a march on Ottawa.
>
> As something like 1,800 SIU members milled around the environs of Parliament, I spent several hours in the crowd talking to seamen. From every man with whom I raised the issue of Banks' excessive spending and total use of his author-ity as president, I got an approving, not a critical response. They wanted their chief to have the perquisites and symbols of a tycoon. What use was a leader if he could not be absolute?

Reason copes with reality, but morality is mauled by it. Reason is suspect of morality.

Furthermore, man, for all his intelligence, has not been able to decide whether moralities are societal rules that have somehow historically made it, or whether there is, in some sense or other, an absolute morality to which men ought to aspire regardless of societal rules and custom. Reason has not been able to fathom morality.

So the moral person, suffering the ravages of morality, is not even convinced the burden is worth carrying. The pathos is palpable. The psychic damage is real; alienation is real. For academics and teachers, a privileged elite cocooned from the ravages of competition, to promote and engage in moral education in schools, in the very institution which first separates out winners from losers, which initiates children into the fact and pressures of competition—does one laugh or cry? Does one rage or throw up one's hands?

> When I am not being "handled" by a process person, from whence does my sense of human solidarity derive, my sense that we—fellow citizens—are part of each other? Not from need of, or joy in, my neighbour, not from intimations of shared mortality. My sense of human solidarity is grounded in torment: in a recognition that the need to be ruthless rules us all and that practically nobody accepts the obligation to be mean.
>
> The banner above me, above the cabbie, above the orthodontist, states the unity of mankind in the imperative Dog eat Dog, and I despise this banner, and yet I know that I must, you must, he must, all must beat each other to the light. And I know that none can run this wretched race unless wary, unless skilled in the arts of denial and doubt. . . . Is it not "a problem for schooling" that parent and child in the present culture are closest when together they see through the lie?
>
> Together my daughter and I before the box see that the happy fellow singing "I smell good" is a deceit. We see that America the Beautiful isn't, we see that Jefferson owned slaves, we see that cynical disbelief is, like the shared bitterness at the unremittingness of competition, among the firmest of the blessed ties that bind. And it follows, given this grain of feeling, that while a voice or face in the classroom or flip chart may hold that fairness is good, that the weak and strong must know and value each other, that those who pollute the mind with falsehood deserve and will receive punishment, that life-meaning and enhancement flow from the mastery of the powers of discrimination, the refining of sensitivity, the development of love for beauty and for truth and for each other—while a voice may "stand for" these "verities", I know, we all know, all that this voice is producing is at best only a theatre of hypocrisy: the school in its organization, its form, its essential interior life, is no more supportive of such truths than the friendly Exxon station at the corner, or than I myself am, once the party has ended and I am back on the road. . . . As long as we're bemused with

"alternative devices" and with visions of our own inner selves as instinctively embracing and unguarded, we hide out from the essential continuity of school values and community values; as long as we hold that the "conscience of the others must be pricked", we cannot hope to know our secret opposing selves, the enemies of true learning. (De Mott)

I conclude with four thoughts:

1. Academics who one way or another get across the idea that there is no tension between reason and morality, are a menace.

2. Teachers, especially school counsellors, who don't understand and deeply feel the tensions, conflicts and despairs engendered by the clash of morality and the realities of our society, are a menace.

3. Perhaps we have only demonstrated the moral superiority of a Marxist-type society over democratic-capitalistic society. I wish I could really believe this. Occasionally I do.

4. The price of moral education in North American schools is heavy. But the price of immoral or amoral education would seem to be even worse.

References

Camus, A. *The Myth of Sisyphus and Other Essays*. N. York: Vintage Books, 1955.

DeMott, B. "Hot-Air Meeting" in *Harper's* #251, July, 1973.

Chapter 5

Education for Democracy

Most countries don't give a second thought about using the schools to engender in the young respect for their own particular social systems. Not only are we reluctant to do this in Canada, we actually undermine respect for our political system by holding up for appreciation a false view of that system, a fairy-tale view. Just as John is a bit hurt when he learns that Santa Claus is really only grumpy Dad, so young people are hurt when they find our way of life to be harsher than the fairy story portrayed. The student rebellions of the 60's, and now the current cynicism among students, are products, I believe, of this moving from fairy tale to reality. But Canadian democracy as we know it, as it actually is, is worthy of respect and appreciation, and we have no reason to be bashful about using the schools to engender such respect.

By "democracy" I mean parliamentary government as we know it (laws and policy decisions made by a majority of elected representatives; elections by secret ballot every five years), and liberties as we know them (subject to law: freedom of assembly, speech, religion, media; freedom to dissent). I believe that there are three main reasons why we do so little to engender this respect. Firstly, "engender respect" smacks of indoctrination, which latter is deemed, correctly I think, to be anti-democratic, to be totalitarian. In short, some hold that it is not democratic to engender respect for democracy. Secondly, many greatly respect "true" (or "real" or "genuine") democracy, but are very unhappy with the democracy we actually have, judging it to be little more than a sham version of the real thing. Lastly, some believe that talk of democracy in schools will militate against teachers taking a strong leadership stance and against the attainment of high standards: teachers would be unwilling, it is feared, to be demanding, since a demanding leader is held to be authoritarian (i.e. non-democratic) and would teach to the average ability level, or the lowest, lest the schools become elitist (i.e. non-democratic). All three reasons are flawed. Furthermore, the errors are pernicious, not benign.

Democracy is not a doctrine. It makes no truth claims, neither does it make moral claims, thus standing in stark contrast with religions and ideologies. Democracy is essentially an amoral decision-making process. It can throw up any decision, be it deemed moral or immoral, be it based on truth or falsity. Indeed, inasmuch as moral notions are neither justified nor discredited by majority vote (rape would not be rendered moral by receiving majority approval), it is not surprising that democracy and morality live in a tense stand-off. Democracy does not claim that the majority is right, only that decisions have to be made and that, given respect for individual freedom of thought and expression, democracy is the best (most open-to-change) way of arriving at those decisions.

Furthermore, democracy can be rationally defended—that is, it does not need to be inculcated. Our democracy is the deliberate refusal to put too much power in too few hands for too long, which is to say it has a well-founded fear of oppression by those in power. At the same time, democracy recognizes the need for a law-making, policy-making, effective government, which is to say it also has a well-founded fear of anarchy. Democracy allows hard decisions to be made in the face of opposition without suppressing opposition; it allows social stability along with the continuous possibility of change; it accomplishes changes in power without a tank in sight; and it embraces universal education since it has already decided to accept dissent, not suppress it. Moreover, history has shown that this democracy works; it is not merely a utopian dream. For a society which chooses not to repress minority groups or freedom of thought in general, thus acknowledging and expecting conflicts in value, democracy is clearly the best way of governing.

Thus, to engender respect for democracy as we know it is not to indoctrinate. Democracy is not a doctrine, and respect will be born of citing good reasons for this respect.

To those who respect "true" democracy but are horrified by the democracy we have, I must say that defining democracy in terms of equality, brotherhood, and freedom (which is how such people usually do define it) is nothing but a cruel hoax.

Our democracy has always been hard-headed about the need for effective government, that is, about the need for some people to be in power over others; and that is to say that there will not be equality of power. Democracy is, to high degree, the tyranny of the majority. What little equality there is, is generated by the freedoms embraced by our democracy, by the opportunity to assert one's views. Any vision of democracy that eliminates the need for effective government is utopian and perverse; non-government, which is to say anarchy, is not a viable mode of social life.

Democracy places its money upon the principle of competition, and hence streams people into winners and losers rather than into brotherhood. Conflict is at the heart of democracy, captured and crystallized in the institution of parliament where political parties struggle for power before a judging populace. In democratic systems of justice the courtroom is an arena of conflict between two lawyers, each struggling for victory before a judging populace jury. Furthermore, it is no accident that most democracies still cling to a high degree of capitalism, a system wherein producers compete for markets before a buying populace. Any vision of democracy that exalts equality and brotherly love has to deny competition and conflict, and thus falls into the arms of totalitarianism. Far from being "true democracy", such visions sever all connection with real democracy.

As for an idealized democratic dream of freedom, no society will willingly let others violently overthrow it. "Absolute freedom" is strictly speaking, and practically speaking, nonsense. Democracy embodies the rule of law, holding law to be our best guarantee of personal liberties. Any vision of democracy that eliminates the rule of law, and rails against police and R.C.M.P., falls into the arms of either totalitarianism or anarchy. Either way, individual liberties will suffer loss.

In short, "true democracy" is utopian and non-democratic. The democracy which we have does work, does sustain large measures of personal freedom, can throw up decisions which will seek to reduce inequalities, does not forbid brotherly love, and mildly supports brotherhood in the sense that democracy forbids lawlessness and believes all should have their say. But democracy is essentially conflict. The freedoms enshrined in democracy live in dynamic tension with the need for law and policy. Freedoms mean conflict, since unoppressed people who have access to education will differ greatly in their beliefs and ambitions. I have said that "true democracy" as the confluence of equality, brotherhood and freedom is nothing but a cruel hoax, and not something we should foist upon the children in our schools. Yet some notable educators foster such a hoax:

> When the school introduces and trains each child of society into membership within such a little community, saturating

him with the spirit of service, and providing him with the instruments of effective self-direction, we shall have the deepest and best guarantee of a larger society which is worthy, lovely and harmonious. (Dewey, p. 49)

For anyone who takes democracy seriously, the claims of the ideals of freedom, equality and fraternity must all be respected in making practical policies. . . . A theory in which any of these ideals is either given overwhelming significance or virtually ignored can hardly claim to be democratic. It would not simply be a version of democracy, but a different kind of political theory altogether. (Crittendon, p. 149)

Finally, the notion that democracy militates against high standards or strong teacher leadership is absurd. Far from being a levelling process, democracy embodies the struggle for supremacy; the spoils go to the capable. And democracy assumes strong leadership inasmuch as it assumes strong government. Democracy is also, however, the attempt to prevent oppression, and hence education should be our very best effort at bringing all children to the limits of their potential. This, obviously, does not mean holding bright students back, nor does it mean weak teachers; it means exactly the opposite. In short, there is nothing within democracy that militates against high standards. Democracy is not anti-intellectual or anti-expert; democracy is not foolish.

Thus there are no good reasons for refraining from engendering in our young people respect for democracy as we know it. Our democracy does merit appreciation. Because we have strong government we bask in the benefits of social order; we do not fear to walk the streets. Changes in power within our society occur without a drop of blood spilt. We enjoy freedom of thought, of assembly, of faith; our children have access to self-development through the public education system; we have access to information and opinions through non-censored media; and we have freedom to dissent. There is the continuous possibility of social change, which is to say that there is always the possibility of improvement. If this does not merit appreciation and respect, what does?

In sum, the democracy that we have is the attempt to create a viable way of life that actively supports diversity and dares to flirt with dissent. Because it is not a doctrine and does not claim to be moral, it need not rest its case on indoctrination, but rather can embrace education and stand upon reasons. Rather than rail against its lack of divine perfection, let us appreciate democracy, the real democracy that we do have, as a spectacular human achievement the like of which may never again be seen in human history. Let us as individuals seek to improve the decisions the democratic process makes. Let us teach our children, in the schools, to respect it, messy, unjust and conflict-ridden though it be. Mess is the price of freedom.

Rebelling students in the sixties claimed that the only difference between themselves and the adult establishment was that unlike their elders they really believed in the democracy of equality and brotherhood that the elders had held up to them, and what they saw around them was not really democracy. But what they saw around them really was democracy. What they had been taught was a lie, a cruel hoax.

References

Dewey, J. "The School and Society" in *Dewey on Education*, ed. M. Dworkin, New York: Teachers College Press, Columbia University, 1959.

Crittendon, B. *Education and Social Ideals*. Ontario: Longman Canada Ltd., 1973.

Chapter 6

Students' Rights and Student Power
A Philosophical Perspective

In many parts of North America in the sixties and seventies students militantly demanded the right to do this, that and the other. On behalf of those rights, students organized themselves into power groups and/or infiltrated decision-making positions of power. Most education administrators viewed this militancy with alarm.

The philosopher has a certain unique perspective. Like the spotter in the spotter's box, high above the football field, the philosopher from his ivory tower sees the contest as a whole. The philosopher, in presenting his perspective, is not urging students to cease pursuing their rights, nor is he urging administrators to cease pursuing their rights, he only urges that his perspective is a valuable one. The philosopher is on the side of man, not groups of men, since he assumes that truth is valuable in and of itself, which is to say that it is of value to all. The following, we here claim, is the truth about the pursuit of students' rights and student power.

******

Students' rights and student power. Rights and power. Cats and dogs. The title suggests a wide separation between "rights" and "power"; like "cats" and "dogs", we sometimes find "rights" and "power" together, as in this essay's title, but we could just as easily find them, and consider them, apart. I wish to show that rights and power are locked together such that rights cannot be considered apart from power; the word "and" in the phrase "rights and power" is misleading.

When claiming and striving for a right, we are essentially seeking a 'power to do X'. If parity on governing councils in universities is viewed by students as their right, and they pursue this right, then they are pursuing a certain 'freedom to do', a certain 'power to do'. Furthermore, they are seeking this freedom, this power, from others whose power is such that they need their assent or their removal from positions of power. That is, claiming a right assumes a prevailing power block which is preventing the claimants from doing that which they judge they have a right to do. The more helpless, powerless, the claimants feel in the face of the power they are confronting, the more strident will be their calls and the more attractive will be the use of violence since if one cannot obtain assent to do x, then one can only wrest assent by crushing, one way or another, those who stand in the way. The pursuit of rights, then, is a pursuit of a certain freedom-to-do, a certain power-to-do, against a prevailing power that is currently preventing that freedom, that power-to-do.

In pursuing a right we are pursuing a *certain* freedom, a *certain* power-to-do, not just any old freedom, not just any old power. Pursuing the freedom to use Dad's car on a Saturday night or to borrow a colleague's typewriter is not normally seen as pursuing a right. The distinctive feature of a right is that this freedom-to-do is backed by morality. That is, in pursuing a right, we judge ourselves to be in the right; we appeal to morality for support: we use words like "good", "moral", and phrases like "ought to be" to lend force to our cause, to lend it power. And in so appealing to morality,[1] assuming sincerity, we prove, once again, how much power moral conceptions can have over people. People have doused themselves with gasoline and burned themselves to death in order to serve the cause of the moral; people have refrained from wealth because "stealing is wrong", have fallen in love and refused to make love because "disloyalty is wrong" or "being hurtful to another is wrong", and students, in battling administrators, have put careers on the line, have stuck their necks out, because "these are our rights". Some people are driven by moral conceptions, are virtually helpless before their power.

Furthermore, these moral conceptions were born of a relationship of power. We learn the use of moral discourse, of words like "good", "right", and such, from others. As children we are helpless before those powerful significant others who initiate us into language. Piaget maintained that children go through a stage of naive realism:[2] I teach my young child "That sort of thing is a tree", and I teach him "That sort of action is good, morally good", and in my child's mind the one is as incontestable as the other. If I am taught that x y z are morally good, then this forms my valuation base. My valuation base comes from without, hence the 'air' of objectivity that moral goods have, the 'I ought' as opposed to 'I want'. Max Stirner's intent was to overthrow even the very form of morality since only thus could a man free himself from the domination of others.[3] Because I here hold, following Jean-Paul Sartre, that man is, ontologically, freedom, that the values that shape him he freely sustains,[4] I hold that he can cast off all moral conceptions of the order "X is good. All ought to do X". Thus he becomes immoral (violates, in his own eyes, his own moral conceptions) or amoral (rejects the very conception of morality). But if he clings to certain conceptions "X is good. All ought to do X", he cannot have wiped out, and cannot wipe out, his total valuation base since to do so, amongst other things, would be to wipe out all sense of 'ought'; if he remains moral, he either keeps all his learned moral values, jettisons some and hierarchizes others, hierarchizes one, downplays some and jettisons some— anything but drops all learned values. The chief way the historical moral chain can be broken is for one person (or persons), who wants people to behave a certain way, to teach those people a new set of moral values and for them to accept, childlike, those values as 'true'. Since adults are not generally childlike, fear and/or faith are good strategies to 'impress' the lesson. Morality is the language of man's domination of man, of one man's power over another, of individual-social control.[5] It is the subtlest domination since the one dominating is entirely hidden behind the apparently factual "X is good. All ought to do X"; inasmuch and insofar as morality presents itself in factual guise[6] ("X is good," is a declarative sentence, a statement) it is deception.[7] People who hold moral values necessarily reflect, to some degree or other, the impress of childhood/childlike training.[8] Our moral conceptions are born of a contingent power relationship wherein we were, at that time, overwhelmed.

Nietzsche posited a total freedom with regard to valuing: values are a creation of man, therefore I, being a man, can throw off the burden of imposed values and create a brand new set of values. Thus he talks of picking up pretty shells on the beach:

> Alas, my friends! May *yourself* be in your deed as a mother is in her child; I would fain this were *your* definition of virtue!
>
> Verily, perchance I have taken from you an hundred definitions and the dearest plaything of your virtue; and now are ye wroth with me as children are.
>
> They played on the seashore—then came a wave and swept all their toys away into the deep: now they weep.
>
> But this same wave shall bring them new playthings and cast new coloured shells at their feet.

> Thus shall they be comforted; and like them ye also, my
> friends, shall have your comforts—and new coloured shells!
> (p. 86)

This freedom to start a morality all over again I am precisely denying. What will make the coloured shells appeal to me, to carry on the analogy, will be a function of childhood, or childlike, learning. I am neither the total victim of childhood learning nor am I, in a sense, utterly free from it. I am not total victim since I can reject any or all moral values. I am not totally free of it inasmuch as I, qua one who sincerely holds to moral values, cannot sincerely hold to a self-created, self-chosen completely new morality (i.e. to a morality totally distinct from the one learned), and could only sincerely hold to a completely new morality presented by another if I became as a child before him, that is, accepted his word unquestioningly. Thus I maintain that Nietzsche was more correct when he talked of morality in terms of tyranny and childlikeness:

> To create new values—even the Lion is not able to do this:
> but to create for himself freedom for new creation, for this
> the Lion's strength is sufficient.
>   To create for himself freedom and an holy *Nay* even to
> duty: therefore, my brethren, is there need of the Lion.
>   To take for himself the right to new values—that is the
> most terrible of takings for a burden-bearing and reverent
> spirit. Verily, for such it is a robbery and the work of a beast of
> prey.
>   Once it loved as Holiest 'Thou shalt': now must it discern
> illusion and tyranny even in its Holiest, that it may snatch
> freedom from its love: for this there is need of the Lion.
>   But tell me, my brethren, what can the Child do which
> even the Lion could not? Why must the ravaging Lion yet
> become a Child?
>   The Child is innocence and oblivion, a new beginning, a
> play, a self-rolling wheel, a primal motion, an holy yea-saying.
> (p. 20)

Born of a power relationship, driven by the power of moral conceptions to seek or wrest power-to-do from those who now hold power, the pursuit of rights further demands the exercise of power in order to succeed. The pursuit of rights is not like the pursuit of wants. One cannot easily shelve rights because to do so would be "wrong", whereas one can quite easily shelve borrowing Dad's car or borrowing a colleague's typewriter. Moral values demand action on our part and if we fail to act they accuse us of evil. To say "X is right" and do nothing to establish X in the world is to be open to the charge of insincerity, hypocrisy, lying, or at the very least, cowardice. The accusing voice, whether from within or without, will say: "You say 'X is right, is good, it ought to be' but your lack of action on behalf of X shows you do not really accept it as such. By doing nothing, or very little, you support the present situation, which is to say that you are supporting not-X in the world, which is to say that you are working against X, hence I can accuse you of insincerity when you say 'X is good'." Moral conceptions drive us to action, drive us to use power in order to establish the right and good we are claiming. Thus it is that righteous revolutionaries are made.

Born of a power relationship, driven by the power of moral conceptions to seek or wrest power to do X from those who currently hold power and are blocking X, the claiming of a right, then, involves the exercise of power since the thrust, being moral, is urgent, is serious, is no light matter.

There are two main ways to achieve rights from a power group. One way, a peaceful (more or less) way, is to play on the power group's values. If a minority group is pursuing a right to X, then we can assume that the prevailing power group either values not-X or does not value X. But few people, if any, hold just one value. Hence you play on other values that they hold, and show them that by refusing to value X they actually thwart, to some degree or other, at least one of their other values. This puts them in a quandary and softens them up. This is an instance of moral argument. If, however, they value not-X and are not willing to compromise it to any degree either because none of their other values impinge on it or despite the fact that other of their values impinge on it, then you must resort to the use of fear and/or force: you must overpower them. Values and fear are two dominant, over-riding driving forces in man; to move a man you play on one or the other; play on both, and he will be virtually helpless before you.

In pursuing rights, students are in a unique position for if arguments fail they can easily put pressure on a teacher.

Teachers know, they have all been taught by colleges of education and writers in the field of education, that student interest is the key to achieving the goal of education, namely students learning and appreciating. Students, by the very simple manoeuvre of refusing to interest themselves in whatever the educational institution is trying to help them learn and appreciate, can bring tremendous pressure to bear on the teacher; any teacher's students can render him helpless before them any time by simply walking out on him physically or mentally. The news that no learning or appreciating is going on in Mr. So and So's classes could be spread abroad in appropriate places (the ears of administrators 'over' him, parents, news media) but would in any case soon get around. Even if the teacher could withstand the psychological pressure he is, qua teacher, a failure. Moreover, by promising co-operation if the teacher will grant their rights, the students play on the teacher's values and thus totally undermine the teacher's position. The stark truth-cum-dilemma of teaching is that what the teacher, qua teacher, is after, only another, the student, can deliver. A teacher's success is in the hands of another. If man is, ontologically, freedom then there can be no guarantee of success in teaching regardless of how lucid or vital the teaching or how careful one is never to go beyond the abilities of the students.

Dewey sought success in bringing about student growth by utilizing student interests. Because, then, the student values what is going on in the classroom, because it strikes him as worthwhile, and because he is able, we assume, to successfully do whatever is involved, he has no motive to challenge and defy the teacher— hence Dewey's claim that the teacher need not be an external boss.[9] If a student did defy such a teacher, and in so doing disrupted the class, Dewey would remove him from the class and admit failure, but Dewey found it difficult to accept that the good teacher could not tie in to the experience and interests of the student.[10] Illich, however, goes the whole no-boss route and hence cannot even accept compulsory schooling.[11] The Illich teacher teaches only by consent, only what students want or accept. So long as the teacher has the necessary knowledge and/or ability, he cannot fail since there can be no question of disinterest or value clash—to teach is essentially to serve the interests and values of others. But once a society and/or individual teacher insists on some values of their own, (e.g. a society enforces school attendance or a teacher insists that his students write exams or do so-and-so) the possibility of value clash and/or disinterest arises, and hence the possibility of teacher failure. If students force, as an act of freedom, a teacher's failure, his job and mental health are threatened. Thus, inasmuch as qua teacher I have an aim of students learning and/or appreciating, and inasmuch as qua average person I need money for day-to-day living, I am a sitting duck for students who are out to change what, and how, I am teaching. To gain their freedom-to-do, to gain power, they can play on my values qua teacher and on my fear of loss of bread for me and mine. I am very much at their mercy.

Students, then, *working as a group*, can, by simply refusing to learn-appreciate, by turning themselves off, put crushing pressure on any teacher and any educational system. The difficulty the students have is in getting together and working together as a group: students are not agreed on what their rights, specifically, are; students have other values that are violated, to some degree or other, by certain rights and hence the force of the right is weakened and/or dissipated in their case, and their enthusiasm for action soon wanes; some students could not care less about rights or moral conceptions of any sort, they simply want the material rewards offered by the system; some students just are interested, just do want to learn and appreciate, and will not fight the institution which helps them, albeit in typically imperfect human fashion, in their quest. Discipline is the essence of power, but discipline is hard to come by. It usually has to be imposed by someone who has grabbed power.

Human history is a matrix of energies, of powers, an interlocking, overlapping series of pressures and pulls, with overriding power slipping from here to there to there, ad infinitum. The contingency of human history, individual or collective, is hidden, transformed, by such shining words as "rights". Morality appears to inject a firm reference point, a guiding star, a firm purpose, a 'this at least is important whatever else comes and goes'. But from a neutral observer's point of view, from the spotter's box, morality is seen to be the chief means whereby one person shapes, and is usually shaped by, an other. Right flows from might. But many, indeed most, are not neutral observers. So long as one is engaged and engrossed in the game, the rules (and their development) are of paramount importance, infractions are wrong, and players can argue over 'oughts' and reason carry the day. If players have at least one common objective at the time of argument, there is possibility that reason will decide the argument since reason will be able to weigh consequences, devise strategies, etc., in the service of that end. Thus reason too appears to inject a firm reference point. But if the common objective is of the sort "X is good. All ought to do X" then it must be insisted that this was learned, it was not a product of reason unless the one citing the moral judgement clearly sees it merely as a strategy to get what he merely *wants*.

It is not, then, that reason cannot argue moral issues, it is that moral issues, in the *final* analysis, are prior to reason. Thus reasoning and sensible people can disagree on moral issues e.g. over abortion. We learn a number of moral values and any one of them, given a measure of consensus, can provide base for a reasonable argument; moral arguing is a fairly common occurrence. Moreover survival is, practically speaking, a common objective, and hence freedom from violence is, practically speaking, a common objective, and hence law is, practically speaking, a common objective, and actual bodies of law do follow the morality of the societies of which they are law, hence are largely pervaded by it and often buttressed by it (that is, children are taught "It is immoral to break the law"). Thus one can always find good reasons for "X is good. All ought to do X" if it reflects your values and/or wants and/or helps you to survive; reason will appear to be, and in a sense is, all. But law is clearly a society's strategy designed to facilitate the objectives of some or all of those in society, whereas morality claims, in its very language, not to be a strategy ("Justice is good" is not a strategy—one should be just whether or not it advances one's objectives; morality imposes a supreme objective to which all other objectives should bow; it demands that reason provide strategies for it but it itself is not a strategy, curbing and shaping objectives rather than serving them), and claims to be above any society ("Killing for fun is wrong"—no society should be exempted from this judgement; morality expects to be served, not to serve). Hence, despite all instinct to survive and do what they want, people have willingly died for morality. Thus it is that laws are criticized and disobeyed in the name of morality. Because of its claim to be above the law, morality is the enemy in the very heart of law. The deliberate strategy of using morality to ensure compliance with law bears in it the seeds of its own destruction despite its general overwhelming effectiveness. Law and morality, possibly man's highest achievements, are locked in uneasy dialectic, each ready to crush the authority of the other. Each wields massive power over people. But each is contingent. Each is a consequence of power. 'Right' is in the contingency, not above it; 'Good' is at the heart of the powerplay, not beyond it. History is a function of power groups, not a pure Hegelian Absolute and not a predetermined-in-aim Marxist dialectic.

******

From the spotter's box the game is seen to be rough. People get both manipulated and hurt. Some conclude that life is absurd, which is to say that the game is contrary to the expectations of a rational being; some conclude that life is tragedy; some conclude that if this is a correct description of the game then life is despair; some conclude that there must be something or Someone not open to man's ordinary viewing, something or Someone that escapes the spotter and which in fact makes more sense of the game; some conclude that life is a marvellous free adventure;

some conclude that not to look but rather to play is obviously the wise choice; and some conclude that spotters, and spotting, are destructive of both individual and society and should not be permitted. Whatever the conclusion, different groups continue to fight for their rights.

In the 1980s students claim the right to dress as they please, exceptional students claim the right to specialized education, children with AIDS claim the right to attend school. . . . So human history wends its tortuous way. It is a matrix of energies, the clash of powers. In it there is no firm reference point other than self-assertion. Or so it appears.

Notes

1. By "morality" we will always and only refer to claims of the order "X is good. All ought to do X". That is, we are talking about a language which ties 'good' with 'ought'. This is a working definition sufficient for the purposes of this essay.

2. See J. Piaget, *The Moral Judgement of the Child* (London: Routledge & Kegan Paul, 1932).

3. See M. Stirner, *The Ego and His Own* (New York: Libertarian Book Club Inc., 1963).

4. See J.- P. Sartre, *Being and Nothingness* (New York: Libertarian Book Club Inc., 1963).

5. Cf. ". . . rules should be inculcated with the maximum impressiveness and seriousness. Then they will become not only second nature but also so respected and revered that they will be broken only with feelings of guilt." K. Baier, *The Moral Point of View* (New York: Random House, 65) p. xvii. "Who is there that has never, more or less consciously, noticed that our whole education is calculated to produce *feelings* in us, impart them to us, instead of leaving their production to ourselves however they may turn out? If we hear the name of God, we are to feel veneration; if we hear that of the prince's majesty, it is to be received with reverence, deference, submission; if we hear that of morality, we are to think that we hear something inviolable. . ." M. Stirner, *op. cit.*, p. 66. See also B. F. Skinner, "Some Issues Concerning the Control of Human Behavior", *The Helping Relationship Sourcebook*, eds. Avila, Combs & Purkey (Boston: Allyn & Bacon, 71) p. 68.

6. See Jean-Paul Sartre, *op. cit.*, and R. M. Hare, *The Language of Morals* (London: Oxford University Press, 67), for arguments against the proposition that statements of the order "X is morally good" are factual, that is, essentially descriptive. The writer

considers the combined positions conclusive. Because, however, this essay merely assumes that such statements are not descriptive, the basic claim of the paper is that only a thesis demonstrating that moral propositions are descriptive, and hence true or false, can seriously challenge the thesis here presented.

7. For the force of this deception consider the words of G. E. Moore when forced to reconsider his position of "good" as marking a characteristic: "What is true, I think, is that, when I wrote the *Ethics*, it simply had not occurred to me that in the case of our two men, who assert sincerely, in a 'typically ethical' sense of 'right', and both in the same sense, the one that Brutus' action was right, the other that it was not, the disagreement between them might possibly be merely of that sort (a difference in attitude). Now that Mr. Stevenson has suggested that it may, I do feel uncertain whether it is not merely of that sort. . . . I must say again that I am inclined to think that 'right', in all ethical uses, and of course, 'wrong', 'ought', 'duty' also, are, in this more radical sense, not the names of characteristics at all, that they have merely 'emotive meaning' and no 'cognitive meaning' at all: and if this is true of them it must also be true of 'good', in the sense I have been most concerned with. I am *inclined* to think that this is so, but I am also inclined to think that it is not so; and I do not know which way I am inclined most strongly. If these words, in their ethical uses, have only emotive meaning, or if Mr. Stevenson's view about them is true, then it would seem that all else I am going to say about them must either be nonsense or false (I don't know which). But it does not seem to me that what I am going to say is either nonsense or false; and this, I think, is an additional reason (though, of course, not a conclusive one) for supposing both that they have 'cognitive' meaning, and that Mr. Stevenson's view as to the nature of cognitive meaning is false." "A Reply to my Critics", *Theories of Ethics*, ed. Philippa Foot (London: Oxford University Press, 67) pp. 42, 48–49. Consider also Bertrand Russell's remark "I cannot see how to refute the arguments for the subjectivity of ethical values, but I find myself incapable of believing that all that is wrong with wanton cruelty is that I don't like it." See also W. K. Frankena, "On Saying the Ethical Thing", *Philosophy Today*, ed. J. Gill (New York: Macmillan, 68) pp. 273-278.

8. What we have in mind here is a Sartrean model of transcendence: I can only transcend my past, which is to say that my past 'conditions' my transcending without dictating it. See J.-P. Sartre, *Search for a Method* (New York: Random House, 68), especially pp. 56-65, 100-111.

9. "The mature person, to put it in moral terms, has no right to withhold from the young on given occasions whatever capacity for sympathetic understanding his own experience has given him. No sooner, however, are such things said than there is a tendency to react to the other extreme and take what has been said as a plea for some sort of disguised imposition from outside. It is worthwhile, accordingly, to say something about the way in which the adult can exercise the wisdom his own wider experience gives him without imposing a merely external control." J. Dewey, *Experience and Education* (New York: Macmillan Company, 66) p. 38.

10. See for example, *Ibid*, pp. 56-57.

11. "In fact, healthy students often redouble their resistance to teaching as they find themselves more comprehensively manipulated. This resistance is not due to the authoritarian style of a public school or the seductive style of some free schools, but to the fundamental approach common to all schools—the idea that one person's judgement should determine what and when another person must learn. . . . Deschooling is, therefore, at the root of any movement for human liberation. . . . The totally destructive and constantly progressive nature of obligatory instruction will fulfil its ultimate logic unless we begin to liberate ourselves right now from our pedagogical hubris, our belief that man can do what God cannot, namely manipulate others for their own salvation." I. Illich, *Deschooling Society* (New York: Harper & Row, 1970) p. 60.

References

Nietzsche, F. *Thus Spake Zaruthustra*. London: Dent, 1960.

Chapter 7

Moral Education and Mystery

Current approaches to moral education include programs based on the Values Clarification approach (Raths, 1978; Simon, 1972), on the Reflective Ethics approach (Beck, 1972), on Kohlberg's claim that one attains higher forms of morality by attaining higher levels of reasoning (Kohlberg, 1981), and on direct instruction in virtue. In each case, clarity and precision about morality is either assumed (most forms of direct instruction) or deliberately and carefully pursued (the remaining approaches). Kohlberg, who currently dominates the field, and Beck both emphasize that reason is the necessary springboard to morality. Many forms of direct moral instruction are openly based on clear doctrine founded upon faith and revelation.

The position of Martin Buber on morality and moral education poses a serious challenge to all the above approaches: morality is founded neither upon reason nor faith, and precision is in principle ruled out. In this essay I attempt to explicate Buber's position and use Jean-Paul Sartre as a foil since I am convinced that humankind's deepest hopes and fears find expression in these two philosophies, and that the similarities and contrasts therein are highly illuminating for all concerned with morality and the moral education of our young.

From time immemorial man has wrestled with the question of "the good". Is the good knowable fact, or is it opinion? Is morality merely a serious social fashion, varying over time and space, at heart a social device to shape an individual's behavioural garb? Is it pathetic to be seriously moral since we thus declare ourselves fashioned by others? Or is morality man at his best? If this latter, what scale of values is it that registers "best"? If the history of philosophy proves anything, it proves that morality is elusive, is enigmatic. We have been unable to demonstrate what exactly is good. Furthermore, we are not even exactly sure what is being claimed when something is held to be good. These conspicuous failures may simply mark current ignorance; but it may be that the good emanates from beyond reason, from mystery.

Mystery, as here conceived, refers to that which lies just beyond clear sensibility and rationality; that which cannot be clearly seen, heard or touched, nor probed, nor fully exposed by means of rational argument and/or experimentation. Our society's disregard of mystery is palpable; the knowable and achievable dominate the social consciousness. If mystery was a product of faith, then in respecting the decision of many not to take the step of faith, we would fully accept their disregard of mystery. But mystery is not a matter of faith, rather it is a matter of fact clearly articulated by reason able to plot its own limits. In physics, our most advanced science, the uncertainty principle, much of general relativity where maths has taken man far beyond his ability to conceive, and the inescapable use of paradigms, all conspire to overawe the intellect, and remind man of his limitations. There is no need, however, to appeal to modern science in order to establish mystery.

"Why is there something rather than nothing?" is a venerable question that leaves reason helpless. Beyond reason and clear sensibility lies mystery; beyond clarity lies the dimly felt; beyond explanation lies the inexplicable. Modern versions of moral education stress clarity and precision; the enterprise is not haunted by a sense of ignorance, nor does it speak of mystery. In Martin Buber's conception of morality and moral education, mystery dominates and certainty is balanced by uncertainty. I would like to briefly expound his view.

In order to grasp Buber's portrayal of morality, its nature and how it 'takes hold' of a person (i.e. how one is morally educated), one must understand his notion of responsibility. Morality and responsibility are, for Buber, inextricably interwoven.

Buber's notion of responsibility has four essential features:

1. The decision to respond this way or that to this or that other comes from deep within. That is, there is full consciousness that the decision does not merely reflect what is popular, or unpopular, but that it is genuinely, deeply, my own decision; it does not strike me as arbitrary or careless but rather is a response of my 'whole being'.

2. The decision to respond genuinely, deeply, is born of the sort of experience referred to by Buber as dialogue or communion, wherein I have a heightened awareness of the other that is in some sense lyrical, moving and meaningful. In being open to the world, as opposed to using it, I am addressed by it. I experience "that spark of the soul".

The kindling of the response in that "spark" of the soul, the blazing up of the response, which occurs time and again to the unexpectedly approaching speech, we term responsibility. (Buber, 1961, p. 119)

3. In making my response, I am dominated by a sense of having been entrusted with the other. The other must receive from me an honest, genuine response since the other is 'in my care'. I cannot let the other down; I could not harm the other.

I cannot be answerable without being at the same time answerable for the other as one who is entrusted to me. But thereby a man has decisively entered into relation with otherness; and the basic structure of otherness, in many ways uncanny but never quite unholy or incapable of being hallowed, in which I and the others who meet me in my life are inwoven, is the body politic. (p. 83)

4. My deep, genuine response to that other with whom I am entrusted is the response of doing what is right, what is good. Faced, for example, with the reality of Billy in the classroom, and having been open to him and fleetingly, but dramatically, felt his presence, I have to do the right thing. What I do is what I believe, to the very best of my knowledge and intuition, to be right. I am not able to know intellectually that I am right, but I know I am right. The rightness of my response is, for me "uncertain certainty".

I point to the unknown conscience in the ground of being, which needs to be discovered ever anew, the conscience of the "spark", for the genuine spark is effective also in the single composure of each genuine decision. The certainty produced by this conscience is of course only a personal certainty; it is uncertain certainty...(Buber, 1961, p. 93)

...the human, uncertain and certain truth which is brought forward by his deep conscience...(p. 94)

You cannot devour the truth, it is not served up anywhere in the world; you cannot even gape at it, for it is not an object. And yet...there exists a real relation of the whole human person to the unpossessed, unpossessable truth, and it is completed only in standing its test. (p. 67)

Thus, in encountering the world not in the frame of mind of neutral observer but in the lyrical disturbing manner of dialogue, I encounter an unpossessable truth, the eternal values. I experience them as opposed to learn them; I 'sense' them. I cannot doubt them for they are truth. But intellectually I must doubt the whole experience; intellectually I am certain of nothing; I cannot prove or provide clear evidence for what I have 'learned'.

Morality, then, for Buber, is not an upshot of intellectual training or capability or an act of faith, but of openness to the world where within the spark of dialogue moral truths are 'felt'.

> The life of dialogue is no privilege of intellectual activity like dialectic. It does not begin in the upper story of humanity. It begins no higher than where humanity begins. There are no gifted and ungifted here, but only those who give themselves and those who withhold themselves. And he who gives himself tomorrow is not noted today, even he himself does not know that he has it within himself, that we have it within ourselves, he will just find it, "and finding be amazed". (Buber, 1961, p. 54)

Emerging from strange, lyrical, amazing, fleeting relations with the other, person or thing, morality intermittently flashes on to the world scene in concrete, particular experiences. Morality is not an opinion or social convention. Morality is an unpossessable truth which eludes man's attempt to freeze it into language as a statable, analysable, possessed moral principle; morality eludes reason. Values and mystery are inseparable. This is Buber's position.

I would like, very briefly, to compare and contrast Buber's notion of responsibility with that of Jean-Paul Sartre. The differences are startling, and betoken, for me, man's deepest dilemma.

For Sartre (1966), to be is to choose: man is not a mere puppet of biology or environment. Thus man is responsible for his actions since his actions reflect his own choices. Thus Sartre could appreciate Buber's notion of a decision that was genuinely and deeply one's own.

For Sartre, man is also responsible for all men in the sense that we do influence others by our words and actions, and in the sense that when we declare something to be morally good we in fact legislate for all men. (Sartre, 1948, pp. 28-32) "Honesty is good" means "All ought to be honest". Thus Sartre could appreciate Buber's notion of responsibility to others.

But Sartre's notions of responsibility stem from awareness of his own freedom-to-choose and from intellectual understanding of a moral claim. This is in vivid contrast to Buber whose sense of responsibility stems from a vivid awareness of a specific other, and is not translatable into any sort of moral principle applying to all; the response Buber makes is one *he must* make in that situation,

not one *all ought* to make in similar situations. It is highly significant that Sartre has no concept of lyrical relation with the world.
His entire thesis rests on the assertion that consciousness is a
severance from the world. (Sartre, 1966) To be conscious of a tree
is to be aware that I am not the tree. My subjectivity is radically
severed from your subjectivity; hell is other people who have no
option but to objectify me. This radical distance between me and
the other is in vivid contrast to Buber's dialogue wherein, he
claims, all distance collapses and I know the other wholly, as
subject, but in a non-intellectual, awareness-way of knowing. (I
can intellectually know I am mortal, but stricken by cancer I
'really know' I am mortal, i.e. my awareness is pervaded by the
reality of death. The knowledge gained in dialogue is of this latter
sort.)

Moreover, morality for Sartre is a human creation. He likens it
to a work of art. (Sartre, 1948, pp. 48-50) Like a picture, morality
is neither true nor false, rather it appeals to us or it does not; we
either hang the picture up, as it were, or reject it as unattractive.
Arguments over morality, over what is really good, must therefore always be futile in the way arguments over what is appealing
are futile. There may be scientific truths giving man a measure of
certainty in life, but there are no moral truths on which he can
rely. Man is on his own, faced with making his own moral choices.
Moralities will vary over time and space, and will often conflict.
The upshot, scrupulously traced out by Sartre, is conflict,
anguish, despair and abandonment. (pp. 30 ff.) All of which
stands in stark contrast to Buber's lyrical relation with the other
(dialogue), moral truths, and the meaning and certainty those
truths furnish.

Finally, Sartre maintains that consciousness is desire. (Sartre,
1966, pp. 133 ff.) Consciousness is necessarily haunted by the
desire for being, for completeness, for fulfillment, because consciousness is the lack of being (most easily thought of as consciousness being pure process, unable to self-subsist; if no world, then no
consciousness). All historical moralities betoken this ontological
questing of consciousness for perfection, completeness, for lacking nothing. Yet the quest of consciousness for being-perfection is
futile—if it attained being it would cease to be consciousness.
Thus morality is a tangible reminder that man is a futile passion, is
hopeless desire for an impossible fulfillment/perfection/whole-
ness. Thus Sartre's morality is pervaded by arbitrariness and
futility, whereas Buber's morality embraces moral truths, meaning and mystery. Sartre's morality is born of futile desire, whereas

Buber's morality emerges from the complete absence of desire, from pure openness to the world.

Thus Sartre does not feel entrusted with particular others who blaze up in his world in the mystery of relation, in the lyricism of the aesthetic; rather he intellectually acknowledges that others in general will be influenced by him and therefore he ought to feel the weight of responsibility when making his moral choices. Sartre does, however, agree with Buber's notion of "uncertain certainty": "We heard whole blocks screaming, and we understood that 'evil', fruit of a free and sovereign will, is like 'good', absolute." (Sartre, 1948, p. 248) Sartre's certainty is an index of the depth of his moral commitment, a commitment fuelled by an impossible perfection haunting consciousness; his uncertainty derives from his conviction that morality is merely a personal choice, a created picture. Buber's certainty, on the other hand, derives from moral truths which deep conscience flashes forth in dialogue; his uncertainty derives from the mystery of dialogue, the inability to demonstrate anything.

Thus each attests in his own way to the persistence and vitality of morality in human affairs, and each attests to its elusive, enigmatic quality. The one gives hope that morality betokens a higher, purer order, that morality betokens deep meaning in human affairs. The other insists that life is without meaning, that all is arbitrary and futile. Thus are encapsulated man's deepest hopes and fears.

If we accept Buber, then engaging in moral education by posing dilemmas, discussing value issues and laying out alternatives, becoming clear about ultimate life goals and conflicting values, getting young people to move from one developmental stage to the next, all miss the mark. Morality is not intellectual (though social norms are). I am morally educated, according to Buber, to the extent that I meet a great character and meet the other in dialogue. A great character is one who is unified deep down, who is open, responsive, responsible. Meeting a great character will give me courage to be similarly responsible.

> This is where the educator can begin and should begin. . . .
> He can awaken in young people the courage to shoulder life
> again. He can bring before his pupils the image of a great
> character who denies no answer to life and the world, but
> accepts responsibility for everything essential that he meets.
> (Buber, 1961, p. 145)

And to be open and to encounter the other in dialogue will create in me the sense of entrustedness, of having to do the right thing; it will cause me to sense moral truth, the eternal norms.

Genuine education of character is genuine education for community. In a generation which has had this kind of upbringing the desire will also be kindled to behold again the eternal values, to hear again the language of the eternal norm. He who knows inner unity, the innermost life of which is mystery, learns to honour the mystery in all its forms. . . . A generation which honours the mystery in all its forms will no longer be deserted by eternity. (p. 146)

On this count, then, it is not moral teaching that we need, nor curricular strategies, but rather teachers willing to be open, to dare to go with what emerges from the mysterious dimension of life, to respect mystery. We need teachers who are great characters, able to hold their ground because of some deep personal unity in some way grounded upon moral truth, and willing to genuinely, ingenuously, respond to children with the right response and thus satisfy the felt claim of entrustedness.

This is not to say that direct moral instruction is wrong, that Kohlberg has said nothing useful, or that discussing and reflecting upon values is a waste of time. Similarly, courses in moral education for prospective teachers need not be done away with. Treating morality seriously is always better than acting as if it were of no significance. But just as reason, in mathematics and science, has become aware of its limitations, and just as philosophers acknowledge philosophy to be a quest rather than a conclusion (Carter, 1984), so the enterprise of moral education needs to be sharply reminded that mystery is at its core, that at the heart of morality lie relationships rather than learnable principles, and that example is the supreme 'teacher'. Current moral education must recognize the must, the mystery and the flash, not merely dwell on the ought, clarity, and teaching strategies.

But why believe Buber? Perhaps he is just another sentimentalist who can't face up to the absurdity of existence and the need in society for moral laws in order to give the police less to do. Perhaps he abandoned a clearly articulated religion but couldn't quite let go. I can only offer a personal answer. I am convinced that the 'certain uncertainty' attested to by both Sartre and Buber is phenomenologically accurate, which is to say that you feel it too. Also, having taught the philosophy of Buber for the last twelve years, I am always struck by the impact he has, as if he spoke of deeply felt truths. And it is certainly true that if I have been moved by the beauty of a river, I cannot throw trash into it; moved by the presence of a person, I cannot deceive him or her. It is not at all that I ought not, it is that I *must* not; it is not a matter of obedience to a general principle, but rather a specific feel of the right and good.

And if one still asks if one may be certain of finding what is right on this steep path, once again the answer is No; there is no certainty. There is only a chance; but there is no other. The risk [of openness and genuine, ingenuous responding] does not ensure the truth for us; but it, and it alone, leads to where the breath of truth is to be felt. (Buber, 1961, p. 94)

References

Beck, C. *Ethics*. Toronto: McGraw-Hill Ryerson, 1972.

Buber, M. *Between Man and Man*. London: Collins, 1961.

Carter, E. *Dimensions of Moral Education*. Toronto: University of Toronto Press, 1984. (A good, recent restatement of philosophy as a quest).

Kohlberg, L. *The Philosophy of Moral Development; moral stages and the ideas of justice*. San Francisco: Harper & Row, 1981.

Raths, L., et al. *Values and Teaching*, 2nd edition. Columbus, Ohio: Merrill, 1978.

Sartre, J.-P. *Situations 2*. (Quoted in A. Stern. *Sartre*. New York: Dell Publishing, 1967.)

Simon, S., et al. *Values Clarification: A handbook of practical strategies for teachers and students*. New York: Hart, 1972.

Chapter 8

Punishment, Education and Nihilism

A society is a group of people trying to operate together in a viable and valued way. Laws permit viability and exemplify fundamental values. Living within a frame of written laws appears to be one of man's better social achievements. This is particularly so in a democracy, where there is some hope of changing laws and where law-making is constrained and coloured by an enduring tradition of respect for individual and human rights.

Our society does not flinch from punishing the rapist or habitual swindler; all societies punish those who break the law. By "punish" I here and hereafter mean "blame the offender for the offence and force the offender to undergo unpleasant consequences." To undermine law and respect for law is to undermine society itself. Whilst in the name of a higher, that is, moral law some persons may deliberately and legitimately operate in defiance and contempt of laws, nevertheless, when they in their turn become lawmakers, they too will punish those who break the new laws. In our democratic society, the younger the offender, the lighter the offence and the more mitigating the circumstances, the less unpleasant are the consequences imposed; to believe in law and its enforcement is not to be vicious or sadistic, rather it is to fear anarchy and to value a certain way of living together. It is the rejection of nihilism.

A school is a society. A class is a society. It is remarkable, therefore, that so many teacher educators, teachers and, especially, student teachers avoid the very subject of punishment. For many not even talk of punishment is legitimate; Dreikurs echoes their position: "First, the principle of reward and punishment must be abandoned." (1972, p. 61)

Clearly, a decisive reason for not punishing and for refusing to entertain the very topic of punishment is the belief that people are not responsible for their actions and hence cannot be blamed. A strict behaviouristic view of man maintains that man's behaviour is shaped by genes-stimuli—choice is an illusion as is, therefore, responsibility.

> An experimental analysis shifts the determination of behaviour from autonomous man to the environment—an environment responsible both for the evolution of the species and for the repertoire acquired by each member. (Skinner, 1971, p. 205)

> The experimental analysis of behaviour goes directly to the antecedent causes in the environment. (Skinner, 1974, p. 34)

> Man is a machine in the sense that he is a complex system behaving in lawful ways. (Skinner, 1971, p. 193)

Put simply: man is brain, brain is computer, computer is already programmed by genes, stimuli from conception on are the data fed into the computer, and behaviour is the output; we are not responsible for our behaviour.

Interestingly, one could take the reverse view and still be reluctant to punish. Whereas for Skinner "there is no place in the scientific position for a self as true originator or initiator of action" (1974, p. 248), for Jean-Paul Sartre "for human reality, to be is to choose oneself." (Sartre, 1966, p. 568)

> For us, on the contrary, Adam is not defined by an essence....Adam is defined by the choice of his ends; that is, by the upsurge of an ecstatic temporalization which has nothing in common with the logical order...he chooses to learn what he is by means of ends toward which he projects himself. (Sartre, 1966, p. 603)

> ...this truth—the free choice which a man makes of himself is completely identified with what is called his destiny. (Sartre, 1950, p. 192)

But one chooses not in a vacuum but within a concrete situation:

> There is freedom only in a situation, and there is situation only through freedom. Human-reality everywhere encounters resistance and obstacles which it has not created, but these resistances and obstacles have meaning only in and through the free choice which human-reality is. (Sartre, 1966, p. 629)

Put simply, a man's choices *in his world* define who he is, and a mountain is only an obstacle if he chooses to cross it. The *purely* autonomous person, one who chooses within a vacuum, is a fiction; rather we react to, suffer from and act upon our world. The end result of this line of thinking is that whilst a person is responsible for his or her actions since he or she could always have acted differently, nevertheless the circumstances, the situation, could have been such that no person of good will would wish to *hold* the person responsible, that is, to blame or to punish. If a man's family is starving and he steals the food from my deep-freeze, he is responsible since he could have begged on the streets, let his family starve, or whatever, but I would not blame him for stealing and therefore would not punish him. Because children are lacking in experience and in physical and psychological strength, many teachers have great difficulty in believing that the child should be held responsible for his or her actions even if it is correct that to be is to choose.

On a more intuitive level, teachers generally sense that success in teaching hinges to a great extent upon the phenomenon of rapport. Teachers want a friendly rather than a fearful atmosphere to characterize their classrooms. They want to build good relationships based upon mutual respect. When a teacher punishes, when he or she blames a student for bad behaviour and metes out unpleasant consequences, be they a frown in grade 1, a detention in grade 7 or suspension in grade 12, good relations with the offender, and perhaps with the offender's fellow students, cease temporarily and perhaps permanently. Moreover, teachers fear that punishment may provoke active hostility, a hostility that will hinder learning and might undermine the teacher's influence. Dreikurs speaks for many teachers: "We as teachers must recognize that each child is a unique, dignified human being and have respect for him at all times. Then a feeling of mutual trust can be established. And only in such a situation are teachers able to be really effective in their relationships with students." (1972, p. 67) Thus punishment is seen to be destructive.

Moreover, teachers are well aware that they serve as models. Most wish to model understanding, kindness and reason. To punish is to model the use of power in order to gain compliance. "When the teacher punishes, the child's reaction is 'If the teacher has the right to punish me, I have the right to punish her.' This is a major reason why our classrooms are filled with acts of retaliation." (Dreikurs, 1972, p. 60)

Teachers today are also well aware, thanks largely to the influence of humanistic psychology, of the importance of the student's self-esteem and of the dangers of labelling. To single a child out, to humiliate in even the gentlest of manners, is to endanger self-esteem. To label a child "troublemaker", "deviant", "brat" or whatever is to run the risk of the child accepting the label and living up to it. Very few teachers would agree with Jenny Gray's advice to the teacher faced with a persisting offender: "Spare him no mercy. Lean over him and whisper or speak very quietly in his ear. No one but the culprit should hear what you say. Deliver the nastiest most abusive attack on his character, his personality, and his appearance that you are capable of." (1969, p. 23)

Another reason why teachers recoil from punishing is that they regard it as a sign of their failure as teachers. Good teachers, so the argument goes, gain the interest and attention of the students. Interested, attentive students have neither mind nor time to cause trouble. Poor teachers, unable to gain attention or spark interest, will have discipline problems. Faced with an increasingly undisciplined class, Crawford, in his first year teaching, concluded "their natural curiosity had not been aroused. I tried to spice up my presentations and asked more questions of individuals in the class." (NEA, 1974, p. 87) Blaming themselves therefore rather than the students, these teachers redouble their efforts to teach. In a sense, they punish themselves.

This line of thinking gains further support and clout if augmented with notions of a child's innate curiosity and goodness. If the student has innate curiosity but is inattentive and disruptive, clearly the teacher is failing to tap into it; if the student is innately good but is behaving in an anti-social manner, the cause of this behaviour must lie outside the student. The environment becomes the obvious culprit. The misbehaving child is the victim of a poor classroom environment, a poor home environment, a poor cultural environment, a capitalist society, a poor pattern of reinforcement, or whatever. Once you see the student as victim, punishment becomes unthinkable; the child is not to blame. One must be patient and understanding. One must frame an environment which will release and nourish the interest and goodness within the child. Dreikurs echoes this sort of belief, resting his case on the work of Alfred Adler: "Man is a social being and his main desire is to belong. . . . We should realize that a misbehaving child is only a discouraged child trying to find his place. . . . They [children] actually *want* to be good. Good behaviour on the part of the child springs from his desire to belong. . ." (1972, pp. 8, 32, 61)

I think none of the foregoing reasons for avoiding the practice of punishment is insignificant. Teachers have good reasons for being reluctant to punish. But I believe there are more compelling reasons for being ready and willing to punish, for not feeling badly about punishing. I believe there is no reason at all to avoid the topic of punishment.

If you are a strict behaviourist, you correctly reject the notion of punishment as I defined it because you cannot blame the offender; in behavioural engineering, the behaviourist will, if necessary, use unpleasant consequences to shape behaviour but will term this "negative reinforcement". I here reject the behaviourist position in favour of Sartre's to be is to choose and to choose is to be responsible.

Given this latter view, when we punish we are saying, in particular, "You are a person. You have chosen badly. You can choose to behave better in the future. These unpleasant consequences are evidence of our firm rejection of your behaviour and we hope all this will cause you to reconsider how to behave in the future." In the *final* analysis, there is no greater act of friendship and respect than to remind a person that he or she is not the helpless, hopeless, hapless victim of circumstance, to remind a person that (s)he is a person, a chooser. Punishment may or may not work; bad behaviour may disappear, persist or get worse. Punishment may or may not deter others. Punishment may or may not generate active hostility. In a world of choosers nothing is determined. What is at stake in punishing is the elemental and seminal truth that a person is responsible for his or her actions. This truth is upheld. Since no one chooses in a vacuum, mitigating circumstances are taken into account: one exercises due, but not undue, patience and sympathy. Punishment is not anti-humanistic. Punishment is grounded in celebration of humanness.

Also at stake in punishing are the values being upheld, the violation of which occasions the punishing. The school is the embodiment of society's valuing of education. Every child, we believe, ought to get a humane exposure to knowledge, artistic and technical endeavours, and to basic moral values. So serious are we about this value that we have passed laws enforcing school attendance and enforcing payment of taxes to pay for schools. The teacher is under obligation to maintain control of students so that this exposure can go on under the best possible conditions, and to embody and uphold basic moral values. Just as society, then, cannot totally avoid modelling power since it does have certain value convictions, therefore certain crimes, therefore certain punishments, so too the teacher cannot and should not totally avoid modelling power. Laws are not anti-humanistic, rather they defend human rights and moral values as we best understand these. Laws are ineffectual if not enforced. Punishment is humanistic.

Rapport and friendly relations are indeed of prime importance in the educational enterprise, but repeated bad behaviour is evidence that the friendship and rapport have already broken down. It takes two to have friendship or rapport, and if one has reneged the other's persistence is slightly pathetic and likely ineffectual. If the teacher punishes, this may or may not cause further breakdown in relations, but even if it does the teacher's insistence on control is right since other children, wishing or willing to learn, should not be hampered or prevented by a few ill-behaved students. Power is a human responsibility that cannot and should not be ducked. The self-esteem of the punished child may or may not be hurt temporarily or permanently. It will likely not be permanently hurt if the teacher merely punishes and then moves smartly on, that is, does not hold a grudge. The plus of punishment is that it is short and sharp. Gray agrees: "Take care of the offence *when it happens*. Take care of it *thoroughly*. Then forget it." (1969, p. 24) Thus the dangers of labelling are avoided. If the bad behaviour persists, the offenders *should* feel badly about themselves. They are acting themselves into an accurate label, not being labelled into a pattern of acting.

The idea that the teacher is necessarily to blame if students misbehave is pernicious. The teacher may be to blame, and good teachers are haunted by this very possibility, but equally this may not be the case. Even if one takes the behaviourist view, one should not blame oneself when John persists in misbehaving because, quite apart from the difficulties of blaming anyone for anything, your classroom is but small part of John's environment and but brief part of his history of reinforcement; home, neighbourhood and history may well be calling the behavioural shots. On my view, that to be is to choose within situation, it is always possible that the student will choose against you. Finding the reason for that choice may or may not help. Often people are not sure why they choose—some choose on whim for the hell of it. And on my view, whilst a child is not born evil, he is not born good either. Rather he is born to choose; he is condemned to freedom and responsibility. He is capable of good and evil regardless of how those notions are conceived. To necessarily blame oneself for the actions of others is never warranted.

Dreikurs is interesting since he accepts the child as decision-maker, rejects permissiveness but rejects punishment also, using in its place "natural" or "logical" consequences.

Man is a decision-making organism. He decides what he really wants to do, often without being aware of it. He is not a victim of forces converging on him such as heredity, environment....Discipline is the fulcrum of education. Without discipline both teacher and pupil become unbalanced and very little learning takes place. By using consequences instead of punishment, the teacher allows reality to replace the authority of the adult. (1972, pp. 9, 19, 65)

The essence of using consequences turns out to be that unpleasant consequences express "the reality of the social order, not of the person", involve "no element of moral judgement", "respect the child", distinguish carefully between doer and deed, and the voice is "calm and friendly" (1972, pp. 64, 65); "Consequences permit the child to decide what he can and wants to do with the situation." (1972, p. 65)

In other words, Dreikurs is ready and willing to use unpleasant consequences in order to uphold values and to throw the offender on to his own resources and responsibility, but so anxious is he to respect the child who is, after all, only seeking his place in misguided fashion, he will not blame the child; he rejects anger and any sort of moral blame.

But this is a cop-out. The teacher is hiding behind the social reality. The teacher does not morally blame John for hurting Mary, he merely reminds him that in this school-society such behaviour results in a trip to the principal's office. Behind the teacher, an angry society has made strong moral judgements about what is acceptable and what is not and is ready, willing and organized to impose unpleasant consequences. Moreover, on my view, I am my actions, my choices; a person cannot be successfully separated from his or her actions. On my definition, Dreikurs is punishing but like so many others won't admit it. It's not nice. He wants discipline without tears. He is part of the problem, not the solution.

In somewhat similar fashion, the Ontario Ministry of Education tries to have its cake and eat it too. It wants firm discipline measures but does not want the students' self-esteem hurt: "The Ministry is requesting school boards and principals to ensure that each school has a clear code of student behaviour which will emphasize a sense of self-worth...and also state realistic and effective consequences for failure to live up to it." (Dec. 82, p. 7) In words this is not at all inconsistent, rather it reflects twin desires for good behaviour and self-esteem. But the teacher will have to *live* these desires out in the face of real children. For the teacher, the matter is fraught with tensions and dangers. Punishment is difficult.

We should get it straight: punishment is inevitable and right within any society that is not nihilistic, which values a certain way of living. If you are morally opposed to that way of living you can legitimately condemn the punishment as oppressive, inhumane, fascist or whatever. But you are not opposing punishment in principle. Only the nihilist can do that but, unlike you, he is too busy living by whim and fancy to bother sticking his neck out for some fool cause or other.

We rightly fear giving certain people power to hurt others. We rightly fear unrestrained anger and desires for revenge and cruelty. We rightly are cautious about declaring what is of value. But in the final analysis, punishing is grounded in humanism and is demanded by it.

Punishment is humanism in action.

References

Altmann, H. & Grose, K. *The Teacher and the Trouble-maker*. Calgary: Detselig, 1982.

Bowd, A. *Quiet Please!* Toronto: Gage, 1981.

Docking, J. W. *Control and Discipline in Schools*. London: Harper & Row, 1980.

Dreikurs, R. *Discipline without Tears*. New York: Hawthorn Books, 1972.

Gray, J. *The Teacher's Survival Guide*. Belmont, Ca.: Pitman Learning, 1969.

Jones, V. & Jones, L. *Responsible Classroom Discipline*. Boston: Allyn & Bacon, 1981.

National Education Association. *Discipline in the Classroom, Revised Edition*. Washington, D.C.: NEA, 1974.

Ontario Ministry of Education. Education Ontario, December, 1981.

Peters, R. S. *Ethics and Education*. London: Allen & Unwin, 1966.

Sartre, J.-P. *Being and Nothingness*. New York: Washington Square Press, 1966.

Skinner, B. F. *Beyond Freedom and Dignity*. New York: Vintage Books, 1971. *About Behaviourism*. New York: Vintage Books, 1974.

Chapter 9

Tension in the Classroom

...what else can I desire than to exclude nothing and to learn
how to braid with white thread and black thread a single cord
stretched to the breaking point?...there is an inner way...
(Camus, 1955, p. 144)

An outcome of Camus' considerable and incisive thinking about
human valuing[1] is that in valuing beauty-happiness and justice, he
thereby opts for tension[2], for the stretched cord. Life is the
difficult task of weaving threads of opposing colors: justice
demanded that Camus join in the resistance against Hitler, whilst
beauty-happiness condemned the ugliness of all war. Impaled on
his own values, given the fact of a Hitler, of one with very different
sorts of values, Camus consciously accepts the consequent tension, external and internal. By "external tension" I mean conflict
existing between persons. By "internal tension" I mean conflict
existing within one person.

Camus could have escaped the internal tension by destroying
the polarity that was rending him; he could have fled to the
beauty-happiness pole, shutting out the claims of justice, and
quietly read poetry or drunk in the sunset in German-occupied
France. Or he could have fled to the justice pole, deaf to the
claims of beauty-happiness, and killed the invaders gladly, righteously. Unwilling to silence either pole, he opts for the tension of
living between them. "Isolated beauty ends up simpering" he
writes, "solitary justice ends up oppressing. Whoever aims to
serve one exclusive of the other serves no one, not even himself,
and eventually serves injustice twice." (p. 141)

I believe that good teachers similarly opt for tension, external
and internal, whether they realize it or not. "Good teacher" is
here stipulated to mean "a competent teacher who values what he
is teaching and values whom he is teaching"; a good teacher cares
about his subject and about his students.

Being committed to the value of x, education in general or the
teaching of a particular subject, and of students in general, when

students value y, and especially when they value not-x, the result can only be tension.[3] That I am convinced of the value of music or literature does not ensure that John will be likewise convinced; that I am convinced of the worth of formal education does not entail that Mary is too. Given our multi-cultural and economically stratified society, our democratic belief in the right to dissent and the numerous diversions of a technologically affluent society, value clash in classrooms is virtually inevitable, and so therefore is tension. Even a bad teacher will experience external tensions for it is impossible to please everyone. But the good teacher opts for internal tension also, the stretched cord, the honoring of values which often conflict.[4] External tension, if you are aggressive, can be enjoyable, a challenge; internal tension can only be suffered, puts one at a breaking point.

In upholding the claims of education, then, the teacher will often offend, and sometimes hurt, a student; the good teacher cannot let students merely fool around. But offending and hurting students violates the deep value of prizing students. There is no way out for the good teacher; he must accommodate the tension and honor both poles. If you like, the good teacher cannot be too sensitive ("simpering"), neither can he be too effective ("oppressing"). He must live the tense "inner way".

Consider, for example, the continuing debate in educational circles regarding affective and what could be termed effective development. Many see affective, person(al) development as primary. Such people speak of humanity, of human relationships, of self-concept, of wholeness, of mutuality, trust, openness, warmth, freedom and creativity; the important thing is that John be a secure, growing, creative and sensitive being. It is the prizing of people. Others see effective development as primary. Skills and knowledge are to be most prized; accomplishment and excellence are of primary value. What counts is what you can do.

Push hard on affective development, and evaluation, for example, becomes nightmarish. For one to evaluate another is already to wipe out mutuality, to set up a distance, and when evaluations are in dispute relationships can be totally destroyed. Evaluation already bespeaks one person shaping another, already bespeaks a certain loss of freedom. Evaluations exert pressure and produce anxieties, thus working against sensitive and caring human relationships. To fail or do badly can be emotionally bruising, can lead to a loss of self-confidence; separating students into winners and losers can tend toward perpetual separation, a perpetual coldness toward certain others. Push hard enough on affective development and you will refuse to evaluate one person against another, rather you will evaluate each against himself. Push very hard and you will refuse to properly evaluate at all.

Push hard on effective development, and evaluation becomes essential: part of the rigor of virile, effective living, a challenge, a reward. If John is failing and not happy, then he must try harder or recognize a certain lack of ability and/or interest and learn to live with it. We must be realistic, honest, about our capabilities and learn to handle disappointments. John must, like everyone else, find his own brand of excellence and/or worthwhileness, and evaluation helps him in this. One gains nothing by being soft-minded about life. Furthermore, some individuals do not merit trust, let alone love. And to be open and warm is to be non-aggressive, whereas an effective leadership position such as that of the teacher demands a certain amount of pushiness: weak teachers come last.

Insofar as students are solely in quest of education, they will resent evaluation, will see it as anti-educational. They view education as a creative, exploratory journey both meaningful and relevant. They see teachers as people they can turn to should they need help. Anxiety and pressures can only be foreign to, and downright mutilative of, self-motivated quest. Evaluations are seen as hoops the socialized jump through as the ringmaster cracks the whip. Furthermore, the hoops, some will argue, are not merely intellectual hoops, rather they are capitalistic, competitive-society hoops designed to perpetuate the social circus. In the name of education, such students condemn schooling; in the name of mutuality, dignity and freedom they label the schools "shapers" and the teachers "oppressors".

Insofar as students are merely out for a job, out for power, they welcome evaluation since it is the means to success. By honest effort or otherwise they make sure their transcripts have the right letters on them. The quest for self-awareness, critical thinking and creativity bows, if need be, to the primary task of surviving well. Students who stick their necks out, challenging the system, are viewed as pathetic idealists who haven't been able to adjust to the realities of modern life, or as lucky people of independent means. Furthermore, it is the case that certain older people, many of them teachers, do know more than a given young person and hence have some right to evaluate that young person. Furthermore, certain jobs do demand certain competencies.

This polarity, a central one in education,[5] parallels the tension of Camus: to value one is to offend the value of the other. There is no easy answer, only a tension-filled inner way. This tension, occasioned by one who rejects either of the two values, reflects the fundamental tension valuing man *is*: the tension between how things are and how they ought to be, between the real and the ideal, between survival and survival-for-what, between present and future, between power and principle, between job and justice; ultimately between truth and goodness. The Platonic dream of truth, beauty and goodness eventually collapsing into each other is pure illusion. Between the three are severe tensions which moral man must somehow 'exist'. This is the seminal truth that Camus illumines.

The bad teacher can avoid all internal tension by simply fleeing to one pole or the other: the teacher can give up on any learning-type values and simply become the students' attendant, a mere resource person. Or the teacher can so teach that student values are crushed as the teacher becomes a dictator ruling over both subject and students. Teacher as facilitator and teacher as dictator will always haunt the consciousness of good teachers—both are so much easier, so free of internal tension. Moreover, teachers have been taught that tensions in a classroom indicate failure: the teacher has a discipline problem, has failed to motivate the student, has failed to involve the student in a meaningful way, and such-like. Furthermore, the internal tension of the teacher is aggravated by the fact that the teacher is in power relative to the student. The young are morally lucky—they can always see themselves as the wronged, for the other is in power.

Little wonder, then, that being a good teacher is so difficult, demanding and draining. The good teacher, valuing education, necessarily intervenes in the lives of students and necessarily is sensitive to the conflicts this often provokes. The good teacher prizes competence and compassion, control and creativity, excellence and sensitivity, mastery and mutuality. The good teacher honors both education and the individual.

So long as common values, a caring relationship or fear can bind the older and the younger together, so long can the transition from childhood to adulthood, from powerlessness to power, be relatively peaceful. But when a society has many value systems, when there is tension between the older and the younger, when relationships are strained as they are in most large institutions, when society actually prizes critical thinking and self-assertion, and when society refuses to run a system on fear, tension is inevitable and right. In a sense, tension is the educational ideal.

We may now understand why elementary schools are relatively tensionless, and why, on occasion, a secondary school class is 'with it' and one gets that almost inspiring, certainly moving, sense of delightful accomplishment. Elementary schools are relatively tensionless since young children rarely are committed to certain values, being still in the process of establishing them and/or having been told by significant others, mum and dad usually, "Do whatever the teacher says". This 'negative valuing' is aggravated by the fact that they are physically and mentally weak compared to the teacher. By the time students are in secondary school, they have become, or are fast becoming, committed to certain values and/or are willing and able at least not to conform to someone else's values, being in a much stronger position now, both mentally and physically. Nevertheless, occasionally values coalesce; there is a 'coming-together happening', a Woodstock, and the whole group is caught up in the magic of the moment: the 'lesson' has become a beautiful, striking event. But the range of human valuing is so great, and the intensity with which values are held varies so widely, that given all these variables a delightful coalescing can only be a chance happening. Thus when we experience the moving event of a class caught up in the magic of engrossed, harmonious learning, we should not wonder why all classes cannot be like that. One might as well wonder why it is not always 70° with a humidity of 48%.

To hold out to future high school teachers the prospect or goal of delightfully harmonious co-operative learning is to mislead; Dewey misleads. To say that the successful teacher is one who can make learning interesting, or who utilizes student interests, is to hold out an impossible ideal—impossible, that is, over the long haul; learning cannot be made interesting all the time. More realistic is it to say that the successful teacher is one who gains continuing student respect and co-operation. And one gains this by being seen to prize what you are teaching and being seen to prize whom you are teaching and by being seen to cope with the conflicts often engendered thereby.

The good teacher, whether he realizes it or not, is opting for tensions. The good teacher learns to braid with white thread and black thread a single cord, sometimes stretched to breaking point. It is the inner, and honorable, way.

Notes

1. See especially his "The Myth of Sisyphus", *The Myth of Sisyphus and Other Essays*, and his *The Rebel* (N. York: Random House, 1955).

2. See especially his "Return to Tipasa", *The Myth of Sisyphus and Other Essays*, and his "The Just Assassins". *Caligula and Three Other Plays* (N. York: Random House, 1962).

3. In this paper we are not talking about intellectual disagreements which can leave personal relations essentially intact. We are speaking of tension born of acts, of activities. It is comparatively easy to respect a person of differing ideas, but very hard, if not impossible, to respect a person whose actions you deem bad or oppressive (hence the antipathy between decision-makers and intellectuals, between teachers and professors). Internal tension reaches breaking point because one is driven to *act* in conflicting ways.

4. Cf. "It is a great deal to fight while despising war, to accept losing everything while still preferring happiness, to face destruction while cherishing the idea of a higher civilization. That is how we do more than you [the Nazis] because we have to draw on ourselves. You had nothing to conquer in your heart or in your intelligence. We had two enemies, and a military victory was not enough for us, as it was for you who had nothing to overcome." A. Camus, "Letters to a German Friend", *Resistance, Rebellion and Death* (N. York: Random House, 1955) p. 64.

5. Cf. "The emphasis among some community control advocates is often on 'affective' development. By contrast, advocates of a technocratic reform model give more priority to efficiency in terms of time and money, the attainment of intellectual skills, and professionalism. At one level, therefore, the differences between reform proposals are irreconcilable, an important point which contemporary debate obscures." M. Katz, "Present Moment in Education Reform", *Harvard Educational Review*, Vol. 41, No. 3, p. 347.

References

Camus, A. "Return to Tipasa", *The Myth of Sisyphus and Other Essays*. N. York: Random House, 56.

Chapter 10

Deceiving Children

> ...except in very rare circumstances the idea of special learning places where nothing but learning happens no longer seems to me to make any sense at all. The proper place and best place for children to learn whatever they need or want to know is the place where until very recently almost all children learned it—in the world itself, in the mainstream of adult life. ... We made a terrible mistake when (with the best of intentions) we separated children from adults and learning from the rest of life, and one of our most urgent tasks is to take down the barriers we have put up between them and let them come back together. (Holt, 1982, p. 296 ff.)

John Holt, writing here in 1982, has given up on schools in favour of education at home. Schools fail to elicit real learning ("real learning" is learning done out of genuine interest and resulting in lasting understanding) and successfully perpetuate lies; not only have the schools failed in their educational task, they have also failed in their moral task.

> When I was in my last year at school, we seniors stayed around an extra week to cram for college boards. Our ancient-history teacher told us, on the basis of long experience, that we would do well to prepare ourselves to write for twenty minutes on each of a list of fifteen topics that he gave us. ... When the boards came, we found that his list comfortably covered every one of the eight questions we were asked. So we got credit for knowing a great deal about ancient history, which we did not, he got credit for being a good teacher, which he was not, and the school got credit for being, as it was, a good place to go if you wanted to be sure of getting into a prestige college. The fact was that I knew very little about ancient history...two months later I could not have come close to passing the history college boards, or even a much easier test. But who cared?
>
> I have played the game myself. ... It didn't take me long to find out that if I gave my students surprise tests, covering the whole material of the course to date, almost everyone flunked. This made me look bad, and posed problems for the

school. I learned that the only way to get a respectable percentage of decent or even passing grades was to announce tests well in advance, tell in some detail what material they would cover, and hold plenty of advance practice in the kind of questions that would be asked, which is called review. I later learned that teachers do this everywhere. We know that what we are doing is not really honest, but we dare not be the first to stop, and we try to justify or excuse ourselves by saying that, after all, it does no particular harm. But we are wrong; it does great harm. It does harm...because it is dishonest and the students know it....Even children much younger than we were learn that what most teachers want and reward are not knowledge and understanding but the appearance of them. The smart and able ones, at least, come to look on school as something of a racket...(p. 254)

Moreover, the dishonesty is not limited to covering up for the lack of real knowledge.

The fact is that we do not feel an obligation to be truthful to children. We are like managers and manipulators of news in Washington, Moscow....We think it our right and duty, not to tell the truth, but to say whatever will best serve our cause—in this case, the cause of making children grow up into the kind of people we want them to be, thinking whatever we want them to think. We have only to convince ourselves...that a lie will be "better" for the children than the truth, and we will lie. We don't always need even that excuse; we often lie only for our convenience.

Worse yet, we are not honest about ourselves, our own fears, limitations, weaknesses, prejudices, motives. We present ourselves to children as if we were gods, all-knowing, all-powerful, always rational, always just, always right. This is worse than any lie we could tell about ourselves....In a discussion of this in a class of teachers, I once said that I liked some of the kids in my class much more than others and that, without saying which ones I liked best, I had told them so. After all, this is something that children know, whatever we tell them; it is futile to lie about it. Naturally, these teachers were horrified. "What a terrible thing to say!" one said. "I love all the children in my class exactly the same." Nonsense; a teacher who says this is lying, to herself or to others, and probably doesn't like any of the children very much. Not that there is anything wrong with that; plenty of adults don't like children and there is no reason why they should. But the trouble is they feel they should, which makes them feel guilty, which makes them feel resentful, which in turn makes them try to work off their guilt with indulgence and their resentment with subtle cruelties....As we are not honest with them, so we won't let children be honest with us. To begin with, we require them to take part in the fiction that school is a wonderful place...(p. 282)

Radical criticism has lost its steam in the 80s. In the 60s and 70s we loved Neill and his 'be on the side of the child' and 'never compel learning', we read Rousseau who seemed to be some sort of forerunner to Neill, *Education and Ecstasy* sold well and John Holt tirelessly exposed the dark underside of schools. Today we are more realistic, more aware of the one-parent family, the two-working-parents, the need for a safe environment for children and the need to equip children for a harsh adult world where many are unemployed; we believe in schooling.

It is indeed wisdom to face up to reality. And one of the realities we should face up to is that correctly identified by Holt: the extent of deception in schools. Our response, however, is not to reject schools. Rather it is to accept lying as both desirable and inevitable.

The schools, according to critics of Holt's persuasion, are a game. Successful students are those who conform to the rules of the get-it-right-please-the-teacher game and even enjoy it. Unsuccessful students are those who can't or won't play the game. Successful students, now possessing the right credentials, the spoils of the game, go on to do well in life. The unsuccessful students, labelled "dumb" or "deviant" or both, generally grow into their labels, which causes the labels to be applied with increasing frequency, which contributes to their growing more into their labels. . .the end result being that their life chances are severely restricted. Thus schools appear to favour the middle-class child and ill-serve the rest. But the successful children too are stunted and ill-served by the school. Many of them don't even realize that it is all just a game, part of a larger, equally rough and dishonest, adult game. They don't realize they are essentially conformists. And if they do realise, then a conscious loss of integrity, an awareness of life as a "racket", becomes part of the price of growing up. Thus all are losers, except for the adults whose children are nicely babysat. Thus schooling is an insidious, pathetic game, serving adults, and 'destroying' children.

This view fails to recognize that all cultures, and therefore subcultures, are merely social games: each culture is a view of success and failure, fair and foul, umpires and penalties, freedoms and limits, boos and cheers, acceptance and rejection. Because it is only a game it is necessarily permeated with lies and half-truths arising from the fundamental deception that it isn't a game, that it is reality: rules and objectives of the game are felt to be and held to be "right". Schooling is a subgame which will reflect the structure of the larger game. To grow up is to emerge into a game, a reality of praise and pressures. By the time one has realized that the game is simply a human contrivance favouring some and hurting others, it is usually too late to change. We have learned to be realists. Hence the universal staying power of cultures.

The notion that one can break through the game to the 'really real', and thus possibly to the really honest, is, and always has been, tantalizing.

In *The Myth of Sisphus*, Camus determines to build his life only on what is indubitably true, i.e. not on game-related propositions. He sees that cultures are but a species of theatre: each culture equips the child with a stage, a backdrop, lights, applause, criticism and, importantly, a script. Camus is intent on breaking through the local drama to the 'real' human drama lying behind.

> In certain situations, replying "nothing" when asked what one is thinking about...symbolizes that odd state of soul in which the void becomes eloquent, in which the chain of daily gestures is broken, in which the heart vainly seeks the link that will connect it again...the first sign of absurdity.
> It happens that the stage sets collapse: rising, street-car, four hours in the office or the factory, meal, streetcar, four hours of work, meal, sleep, and Monday, Tuesday, Wednesday, Thursday, Friday and Saturday according to the same rhythm—this path is easily followed most of the time. But one day the "why" arises and everything begins in that weariness tinged with amazement. "Begins"—this is important. Weariness comes at the end of the acts of a mechanical life, but at the same time it inaugurates the impulse of consciousness. It awakens consciousness and provokes what follows. What follows is the gradual return into the chain or it is the definitive awakening. (p. 10)

Either one plunges back into the social reality, the only game one knows how to play, or one awakens to the reality of gamelessness, the reality of an absurd world.

> ...in a universe suddenly divested of illusions and lights, man feels an alien, a stranger. His exile is without remedy....This divorce between man and his life, the actor and his setting, is properly the feeling of absurdity. (p. 5)

> The return of consciousness, the escape from everyday sleep, represent the first steps of absurd freedom....The absurd man thus catches sight of a burning and frigid, transparent and limited universe in which nothing is possible but everything given, and beyond which all is collapse and nothingness. (p. 44)

The 'real' drama is far worse than the cultural drama: there are no rules, no familiarity and no point because there is no game.

> I start out here from the principle of his innocence. This
> innocence is to be feared. "Everything is permitted"...
> smacks of the absurd. But on condition that it not be taken in
> its vulgar sense. I don't know whether or not it has been
> sufficiently pointed out that it is not an outburst of relief or of
> joy, but rather a bitter acknowledgement of a fact. The
> certainty of a God giving a meaning to life far surpasses in
> attractiveness the ability to behave badly with impunity. The
> choice would not be hard to make. But there is no choice, and
> that is where the bitterness comes in. (p. 50)

All is permitted. Lying is, therefore, permitted. Unable to
accept this unhappy consequence, Camus proceeds to erect an
ethic based on a universal aesthetic. But a heightened awareness
of the given, brute world, the appreciation of beauty, is hardly the
demand for honesty. The plain fact staring Camus in the face is
that outside of contrived games there are neither rules nor
objectives, only a radical innocence, all given and everything
permitted.

But perhaps Camus got it wrong. Plato seems to have had more
luck. He asserts that beyond the 'real' world we are implicated in
by reason of our senses lies not an absurd, chaotic givenness but
rather an intelligible and harmonious world of 'really real' ideas.

> ...there are many beautiful things and many good. And
> again there is a true beauty, a true good...*that which really is*.
> (*The Republic*)

Evidently the human mind can break through the social game-
drama and attain to The True and The Beautiful. Moreover,
when we do thus break through, wonder of wonders, we discover
that the really real world of eternal universals is harmoniously
knit together by the essence The Good. Our unhappy world of
change, decay, strife, and posturing is a world of shadows which,
however, witnesses to and is proof of the eternal world where
man's mind finally attains dignity and rest. Camus evidently went
wrong somewhere; his fearsome absurdity here gives way to
peace, intelligibility and meaning. Ethics is not only of the fabric
of the really real, it is its crowning glory; the pursuit of The Good
is man's noblest aim.

> ...in the world of knowledge the Idea of good appears last of
> all, and is seen only with an effort; although when seen, it is
> inferred to be the universal author of all things beautiful and
> right, parent of light and of the lord of light in the visible
> world, and the immediate and supreme source of reason and
> truth...(*The Republic*)

Unfortunately, as Plato himself points out, we do have to reckon with this shadow world of appearances. The thinkers, now under the ethical obligation that flows from seeing The Good, must return from the really real world of sun and essences to the shadow world of the cave in order to govern those less well endowed with reason and more endowed with appetites. As an aid to ruling wisely,

> ...the rulers of the State...in their dealings either with enemies or their own citizens, may be allowed to lie for the public good....How then may we devise one of those needful falsehoods...? (*The Republic*)

Evidently lying too can serve, and should be used to serve, the public good.

Martin Buber also believes that one can break through the social game. He asserts that man basically relates in two ways to the world—he uses it for his own purposes (I-It relation) or, bound up in pure relation with it, he lyrically feels its impact and import (I-Thou relation). The world of I-It dwells in the 'unreal'. I-Thou reveals 'true reality'.

> He who takes his stand in relation shares in a reality, that is, in a being that neither merely belongs to him nor merely lies outside him. All reality is an activity in which I share without being able to appropriate for myself. Where there is no sharing there is no reality. Where there is self-appropriation there is no reality. The more direct the contact with the Thou, the fuller is the sharing. The I is real in virtue of its sharing reality. The fuller its sharing the more real it becomes. (Buber, 1958, p. 63)

> Individuality [the I of I-it relations] neither shares in nor obtains any real reality. It differentiates itself from the other and seeks through experiencing and using to appropriate as much of it as it can. This is its dynamic, self-differentiation and appropriation, each exercised on the It within the unreal....The more a man, humanity, is mastered by individuality, the deeper does the I sink into unreality. (p. 64)

I-Thou also reveals meaning and morality. Since relating wholly demands a giving of oneself, the decision not to use and manipulate is crucial to a meaningful, good and really real existence. This giving of oneself, this ingenuous hospitality to the world, this pure receptiveness, is love. Thus love rises above deceit because in I-Thou it breaks through the social, contrived game. Love cannot lie. Loving classrooms would, evidently, rise above the game.

Unfortunately, the world of I-Thou is fleeting. Every Thou must become an It; every lyrical happening must reduce to the categorizable and usable; pure relation must reduce to ordered relationship. In short, the social game must go on. A pure honesty cannot be held on to.

> But this is the exalted melancholy of our fate, that every Thou in our world must become an It. . . . The human being who was even now single and unconditioned, not something lying to hand, only present, not able to be experienced, only able to be fulfilled, has now become a He or She, a sum of qualities, a given quantity with a certain shape. . . . Every Thou in the world is enjoined by its nature to become a thing. . .(p. 16 ff.)

> In this chronicle of solid benefits [benefits of the I-It world] the moments of the Thou appear as strange, lyric and dramatic episodes, seductive and magical. . .loosening the well-tried context. . .shattering security—in short, uncanny moments. . . .It is not possible to live in the bare present. Life would be quite consumed. . .(p. 34)

Thus, while Buber will call for open ingenuousness when dealing with students in a classroom, he will in fact coerce:

> Only in his whole [wholly given] being, in all his spontaneity can the educator truly affect the whole being of his pupil. For educating. . .you do need a man who is wholly alive and able to communicate himself directly to his fellow beings. His aliveness streams out to them and affects them most strongly and purely when he has no thought of affecting them. (Buber, 1947, p. 134)

> When the pupil's confidence has been won, his resistance against being educated gives way to a singular happening: he accepts the educator as a person. He feels he may trust this man, that this man is not making a business out of him, but is taking part in his life, accepting him before desiring to influence him. . . .Confidence, of course, is not won by the strenuous endeavour to win it, but by direct and ingenuous participation in the life of. . .one's pupils. . . .It is not the educational intention but it is the meeting which is educationally fruitful. (p. 135)

> He has to introduce discipline and order, he has to establish law. (p. 142)

But Holt has already rejected coercion because it leads not to confidence but to fear. Moreover, he has acknowledged that one cannot love all children. So the hopes of honesty Buber offered him are dashed.

Nietzsche saw through the social game, but did not see a paralysing absurdity rescued by beauty, nor a harmonious world of eternal realities, nor an elusive world of fleeting pure relations. Getting rid of one game would merely cause another game to rise up. Social games are imposed on geographical areas by those in power with the aim of maintaining or furthering their power. There will always be some sort of social game since man is the will to power and a game serves nicely to keep the masses in order.

> The essential characteristic of a good and healthy aristocracy is that it experiences itself *not* as a function (whether of the monarchy or the commonwealth) but as their meaning and highest justification—that it therefore accepts with a good conscience the sacrifice of untold human beings who, for its sake, must be reduced and lowered to incomplete human beings, to slaves, to instruments. Their fundamental faith simply has to be that society must exist *not* for society's sake but only as the foundation and scaffolding on which a choice type of being is able to raise itself. . . . "Exploitation" does not belong to a corrupt or imperfect and primitive society; it belongs to the *essence* of what lives, as a basic organic function; it is a consequence of the will to power, which is after all the will of life. If this should be an innovation as theory—as a reality it is the *primordial fact* of all history: people ought to be honest. . . .(Nietzsche, 1966, pp. 202, 203)

The Nietzschean individual will not be bound by local game rules; he may well 'snarl' at people he meets. He will certainly lie— why expose oneself to or pretend familiarity with those manipulated by the social game? You will never be understood by them anyway—you are not in their game.

> A great man—a man whom nature has constructed and invented in the grand style—what is he?. . .If he cannot lead, he goes alone; then it can happen that he may snarl at some things he meets on the way. . .he wants no 'sympathetic' heart, but servants, tools; in his intercourse with men he is always intent on making something out of them. He knows he is incommunicable: he finds it tasteless to be familiar; and when he thinks he is, he usually is not. When not speaking to himself, he wears a mask. He rather lies than tells the truth: it requires more spirit and *will*. There is a solitude within him that is inaccessible to praise or blame, his own justice [rule] that is beyond appeal. (Nietzsche, 1967, p. 505)

If the Nietzschean individual gets the chance, he will impose a game that keeps lesser souls in order. The game he imposes, as with all social games, is based on a lie. The rules, which in reality are commands ("X is good or right" means, in fact, "Do X, or else") and therefore cannot be true (or false), are presented and passed on to game-learners, young and old, as statements which are true, all this in the interests of more effective and more extensive control. That ethical systems are merely means of control is attested to by a modern psychologist:

> People living together in groups come to control one another with a technique which is not inappropriately called "ethical". When an individual behaves in a fashion acceptable to the group, he receives admiration, approval, affection, and many other reinforcements which increase the likelihood that he will continue to behave in that fashion. When his behaviour is not acceptable, he is criticised, censured, blamed or otherwise punished. In the first case, the group calls him "good"; in the second, "bad". This practice is so thoroughly ingrained in our culture that we often fail to see that it is a technique of control. Yet we are almost always engaged in such control, even though the reinforcements and punishments are often subtle. (Skinner, 1971, p. 68)

Max Stirner agrees with Nietzsche against Plato:

> To be a man is not to realize the ideal of Man but to present oneself, the individual. I am my species, am without norm, without law, without model, and the like. It is possible that I can make very little out of myself; but this little is everything, and is better than what I allow to be made out of me by the might of others, by the training of custom, religion, the laws, the State. (Stirner, 1963, p. 182)

What Camus shrank from, Nietzsche and Stirner enthusiastically embrace.

Machiavelli, a student of power politics, supports Nietzsche's advocacy of lying:

> Zenephon shows in his Life of Cyrus the necessity of deception to success: the first expedition of Cyrus against the King of Armenia is replete with fraud, and it was deceit alone, and not force, that enabled him to seize that kingdom. And Zenophon draws no other conclusion from it than that a prince who wishes to achieve great things must learn to deceive...(Machiavelli, 1950, p. 319)

> How laudable it is for a prince to keep good faith and live with integrity, and not with astuteness, every one knows. Still, the experience of our times shows those princes to have done great things who have had little regard for good faith and have been able by astuteness to confuse men's brains, and who have ultimately overcome those who have made loyalty their foundation.... It is necessary...to be a great feigner and dissembler. (pp. 63, 64)

Thus Nietzsche, with the support of such as Machiavelli and any modern day politician over the age of twenty-one, holds that deception is part of the logic of power. On this view, Plato's rulers lie because they are rulers and aren't stupid, and Buber's teachers 'lie' because teachers are classroom rulers. Camus' anarchic absurdity is merely the reflective counterpart of civil war—the anarchy that prevails till one game is destroyed and a new game set up. Camus' espousal of beauty to rescue this 'tragedy' would be seen by Nietzsche as effetism of the very worst sort. Rather the individual must virilely impose his own game. Camus, Plato and Buber are evidently quite wrong: there exists no objective, out-side-of-all-games ethic by means of which one can rate social games. Christianity, and indeed most religions, proffer just such a code, but Nietzsche places religions along with political and cultural games—merely a means whereby the masses are manipulated and kept under by the few.

Accepting that lying is part of the logic of power, since teachers are expected to be in control of their classes, teachers will lie. Holt, correctly, in rejecting lying rejects the power relations found in schools. Education at home, he believes, will ensure a caring and respectful type of relationship, not a control-type relationship. Nietzsche would deny this: what will happen is that a parent's game, or child's game, will replace the school game. Let us, however, give Holt the benefit of the doubt and say that in the home a caring relationship will somehow carry the day. Holt is not yet out of the woods. The Grand Inquisitor[1] goes beyond Nietzsche: lying is not only part of the logic of power, it is part of the logic of caring.

In the story of the Grand Inquisitor, told by Ivan, an intellectual, to his brother Aloysha, a gentle man of faith, Christ returns to earth once more, to Seville in Spain in the 16th century. On this occasion, as before, crowds are attracted to Him. The Grand Inquisitor, who yesterday had burned at the stake the enemies of the church, sees the crowd by the cathedral, watches whilst a child is healed, notes the cries and sobs of the crowd, then orders the Stranger to be arrested. There follows, in the dungeon, a defence by the Grand Inquisitor of his actions. Christ never does reply.

The Grand Inquisitor declares that Christ made a big mistake when He first came to earth—instead of impressing the people with a display of power, He set before them only the example of love and freedom. But the man in the street is not capable of living up to Christ's example, rather he needs clear direction.

> Didst Thou forget that man prefers peace, and even death, to freedom of choice in the knowledge of good and evil?

Nothing is more seductive for man than his freedom of conscience, but nothing is a greater cause of suffering. And behold, instead of giving a firm foundation for setting the conscience of man at rest forever, Thou didst choose all that is exceptional, vague and enigmatic; Thou didst choose what was utterly beyond the strength of men, acting as though Thou didst not love them at all—Thou who didst come to give Thy life for them! Instead of taking possession of man's freedom, Thou didst increase it, and burdened the spiritual kingdom of mankind with its sufferings forever. Thou didst desire man's free love, that he should follow Thee freely, enticed and taken captive by Thee. In place of the rigid, ancient law, man must hereafter with free heart decide for himself what is good and evil, having only Thy image before him as his guide. (Dostoevski, 1948, p. 32)

Thou didst not come down from the Cross when they shouted to Thee, mocking and reviling Thee, "Come down from the Cross and we will believe that Thou art He." Thou didst not come down, for again Thou wouldst not enslave man by a miracle, and didst crave faith given freely, not based on miracle. Thou didst crave for free love and not the base raptures of the slave before the might that has overawed him forever. But Thou didst think too highly of men therein, for they are slaves of course, though rebellious by nature. . . .Can he do what Thou didst? By showing him so much respect, Thou didst ask too much from him. . . .Respecting him less, Thou wouldst have asked less of him. That would have been more like love, for his burden would have been lighter. He is weak and vile. (p. 34)

The church has decided to correct Christ's mistakes and take power. We, the church, will declare unequivocally what is right and wrong—thus the people will be able to follow the right and enjoy good conscience, and if they do transgress we'll forgive them anyway. "They will adore us as their saviors. . .we shall have an answer for all." Our law will establish peace and justice.

And all will be happy, all the millions of creatures, except for the hundred thousand who rule over them. For only we, we who guard the mystery, shall be unhappy. (p. 40)

The Grand Inquisitor, and fellow clergy, are unhappy because they haven't a clue what is right and wrong—they merely made it up. They tell their people that the good will inherit eternal life, but actually they haven't a clue about that either. And on the basis of their made-up code, they burn at the stake determined heretics, people who won't accept their authority.

But who cares most for the people? Following Christ, a few get to heaven and the masses, unable to live up to His image, and confused in any case about what is really right and wrong, are condemned. Under the Grand Inquisitor, the masses are happy and a few, namely the rulers, are in mental hell.

> Thou are proud of Thine elect, but Thou hast only the elect, while we give rest to all....But with us all will be happy and will no more rebel, nor destroy one another as under Thy freedom. Oh, we shall persuade them that they will only become free when they renounce their freedom to us and submit to us. And shall we be right or shall we be lying? They will be convinced that we are right, for they will remember the horrors of slavery and confusion to which Thy freedom brought them. Freedom, free thought and science, will lead them into such straits and will bring them face to face with such marvels and insoluble mysteries that some of them, the fierce and rebellious, will destroy themselves; others, rebellious but weak, will destroy one another, while the rest, weak and unhappy, will crawl fawning to our feet and whine to us: "Yes, you were right, you alone possess His mystery, and we come back to you, save us from ourselves!" (p. 38)

> [The Grand Inquisitor] could not shake off his incurable love of humanity. In his old age he reached the clear conviction that...he must follow the advice of the wise spirit [the devil], the dread spirit of death and destruction, and therefore accept lying and deception...deceive them all the way. (p. 43)

In the story, the silent Christ kisses the old man, who releases Christ but orders "Go, and come no more....Come not at all, never, never!"; "The kiss glows in his heart, but the old man adheres to his idea." (p. 45)

If you care, you will lie. Have you read Holt and now aren't sure whether compulsory schooling is a good thing? Never mind, lie. Tell your child that school is the best place he could possibly go to. If you are a teacher, tell your class that computer science will unlock the modern world and lay it at their feet, that music reaches to the very soul of man, that....And when some child persistently rebels, refusing to believe what you have told him, burn him. For the happiness of all, the lie must be maintained; one must not be allowed to undermine the confidence and respect of the masses. Let them know that school rules are right. And when exams come around, or assignments, lie. Scale all the marks up with just enough of a spread to keep it all slightly credible; do whatever is necessary to give them good marks—you surely can't want to hurt their life chances? Surely you love the kids the way they actually are, not just an elite group who will learn regardless?

Do you thereby lose your integrity? In a way, yes. Are you

happy at all of this? Not really, no. But didn't you teach because you 'loved' kids? Do you want to help them or not?

Why, in the story, does Christ kiss the old man? Why does the Inquisitor release Christ? Why does the kiss glow in the old man's heart? Real love, that is, a real, unsentimental caring, is not straightforward, not clear. Lying is part of the logic of love.

It is abundantly clear from reading Holt that he really cares for the children in his class, and indeed, the children of the world; he is genuinely distressed at some of the games most children have to play to survive school. If the Grand Inquisitor is right, if lying is part of the logic of love, then he too will lie:

> How are these high scores achieved? A week or two before the tests, their teachers begin an intensive drilling on all the kinds of problems they will have to do on the test. By the time the tests comes along the children are conditioned, like Pavlov's dog; when they see a certain arrangement of numerals and symbols before them, lights begin to flash, wheels begin to turn, and like robots they go through the answer-getting process, or enough of them to get a halfway decent score. Teachers are not supposed to do this; but they all do. So did I. The school asked me to, rather apologetically, knowing my feeling in such matters, but firmly nonetheless; when children pull down bad test scores there is an instant uproar from the parents. And it makes it hard for the kids when the time comes for them to enter their next schools. Schools being what they are, these poor devils are going to have trouble enough as it is; why make it harder for them by making their abysmal ignorance a matter of public record? So I go along with the practice. But is this a sensible way to carry out the education of our children? (Holt, 1982, p. 260)

Yes, it is, actually. Loving parents, too, will lie. None of us has much of a clue.

Notes

1. See F. Dostoyevsky, *The Brothers Karamazov* (London: Dent, 1968, Vol. 1, p.252ff.). Published separately: *Dostoevski The Grand Inquisitor on the Nature of Man* (N. York: Bobbs-Merrill, 1948).

References

Buber, M. *Between Man and Man*. London: Collins, 1947. *I and Thou*. N. York: Scribner's, 1958.

Camus, A. *The Myth of Sisyphus and Other Essays*. N. York: Random House, 55.

Dostoevski The Grand Inquisitor on the Nature of Man. N. York: Bobbs-Merrill, 1948

Holt, J. *How Children Fail Revised Edition*. N. York: Dell, 1982.

Machiavelli, N. *The Prince and the Discourses*. N. York: Random House, 1950.

Nietzsche, F. *Beyond Good and Evil*. N. York: Random House, 1966. *The Will to Power*. N. York: Random House, 1967.

Skinner, B. F. "Some Issues Concerning the Control of Human Behaviour" in *The Helping Relationship Sourcebook*, eds. Avila, Combs & Purkey, Boston: Allyn and Bacon, 1971.

Stirner, M. *The Ego and His Own*. N. York: Libertarian Book Club, 1963.

Do you know I've been sitting here thinking to myself: that if I didn't believe in life, if I lost faith in the woman I love, lost faith in the order of things, were convinced in fact that everything is a disorderly, damnable and perhaps devil-ridden chaos, if I were struck by every horror of man's disillusionment—still I should want to live and, having once tasted the cup, I would not turn away from it. . . . Though I may not believe in the order of the universe, yet I love the sticky leaves as they open in the spring. . . . I shall steep my soul in my emotion. I love the sticky leaves in spring, the blue sky—that's all it is. It's not a matter of intellect or logic, it's loving with one's inside, with one's stomach. . . . Do you understand. . .?

FYODOR DOSTOYEVSKY